WEATHERING
THE
STORM

All of the principles and practices, techniques and teachings found in this book are based on one philosophy:

"I couldn't wait for success, so I went ahead anyway. If best is possible, good is not good enough!"

WEATHERING THE STORM

Dan Clark

British American Publishing

Published by British American Publishing
3 Cornell Road
Latham, NY 12110
Manufactured in the United States of America

93 92 91 90 89 5 4 3 2 1

Library of Congress Cataloging-in-Publication Data

Clark, Dan, 1955–
    Weathering the Storm / Dan Clark.
        p.   cm.
    ISBN 0-945167-19-9 : $7.95
    1. Teenagers—Conduct of life. I. Title.
BJ1661.C385   1989
158'.1—dc20   89–35662
                                                                        CIP

DEDICATION

To: Kelly Clemente for believing in me. One of the beautiful girls in the world.

To: Dr. Jim Koeninger and Karen Elias for giving me professional opportunities only you could provide. LDI forever!

To: Russ Anderson, Leo Presley, and Zig Ziglar for giving me my start and the confidence to succeed!

To: Dr. Stephen E. Cosgrove, Normand Gibbons, Duane Hiatt, Mike Wells and Dennis Lock for your for your wisdom, amazing knowledge, friendship, sensitive understanding, and especially for your input into this book.

To: My special teachers—Mrs. Dubois (1st and 5th grades), Mrs. Inman (3rd grade), Dr. Moray (4th grade), Mr. Croft (10th grade), Mrs. Smart (11th grade), Mr. Bennett (12th grade), and especially Mr. Tom Thorum (12th grade) who gave me the one break I needed to succeed.

To: My special coaches—Gene Thompson, Dailey Oliver, Din Morris, Ken Clayton, Gordon Wood, John Jefferies, Iman Hales, Dale Simon, Grant Martin, Chuck Banker, Wayne Howard, Ron McBride, and especially Ted Weight, Vince Zimmer, and Tom Gadd who taught me to always get up and go again.

To: Paul and Kristi (hugs for Joshua) for your time, talents, and for typing this manuscript. You are an inspiration to me and my work. I love you.

To: My mother for your support and countless hours helping me to succeed. I love and appreciate you!

To: Samuel Wayne Clark, Sr.—Founder of the multi-million dollar Security National Life Insurance Company and Financial Corporation, Founder of Community Bank & Trust, successful Politician, Government Leader, Farmer, Miner, Horseman Lithographer, Air Force Officer, Church Leader, and most importantly, my Dad! You have taught me that any male can be a father, but it takes a special man to be a Dad! I love you. You're my hero!

Most importantly, To: Kelly, Danny, and Nikola Ann for your never ending love, understanding, countless sacrifices, money, and unquestioned support. I love and need each of you!

Thank you all for "Weathering the Storm."

CONTENTS

WEATHERING THE STORM

The Survival Guide for Teenagers

"Stuff" happens to teenagers: That time of life where it's all we can do to let our parents live at *our* house!

That time in school with report cards—when we come home with four Fs and one D and hope dad says "Son, looks to me like you're spending too much time on one subject!" That time of life when you break up with a girlfriend or boyfriend and, trying to make you feel bad, he or she says, "You'll be sorry—you'll never find another like me!" (I should hope not! Isn't that why you're breaking up?)

That time of life when you make a commitment to your parents to be home by midnight; then you leave the party, run stop signs, take short cuts, race home, squeal into the driveway, sprint in the front door just as the clock strikes twelve, yell "Mom, Dad, I'm home!" and they are not even there!

That time of life when you accidently run into a wall going sixty-five miles an hour and an adult says, "Be a big boy—don't cry."

That time of life when you have a dental appointment and you know it's been two years since your last checkup, so you spend an hour in the bathroom preparing. You use floss, a waterpick, Ajax cleanser, whiteout, and hire a hypnotist to convince you it is not so bad. And what happens? You walk into the smoke-filled dentist's office (the building where all the grinding and screaming is coming from) only to have your confidence shattered by a high-pitched drilling noise that sounds like the dentist missed and decided to go ahead and hang some shelves while he was at it!

That time of life when you realize you live in a little tiny town and convince yourself it's the safest place in America to live. (The Russians will fly over and say, "Wo, we already bombed that—keep going!")

That time of life when you have your dreams but get up and hustle when the alarm goes off.

"STUFF HAPPENS" to adults:

That time of life when brain damage even effects mothers, causing them to yell things like "Don't climb up in that tree. If you fall down and break both your legs, don't come running to me!"

That time of life when you don't realize you're old until you bend over to pick something up and you think "what else could I accomplish while I'm down here?" (Then, you forget why you bent down in the first place!)

That time of life when your age compounds in your mind until you feel you are so old that you won't even buy green bananas!

That time of life when you need attention and try to act more important than you really are. (That's why we have so many people driving around with trailer hitches on their cars and they don't even own anything to pull!)

That time of life when your perspective of exercise has turned to: "The dreaded art of converting big meals and fattening snacks into back strains and pulled muscles by lifting heavy things that don't need to be moved, or running when no one is chasing you!"

"STUFF HAPPENS" to cars:

We all have seen old cars being driven down the road in better condition today than they were back in 1957 when they came off the assembly line. Why? Because, one day, when a man was driving out in the countryside and came across an old, broken down, rusted-out car with no tires or wheels, no windows or upholstery, and a motor that did not work, he did not say "what a piece of junk." He did not look at it merely for what it was. Instead, he looked at this car for what it had the power to become. He took it home, fixed what was broken, and polished it back to perfection.

Human beings are exactly like cars! If we are broken, we too can be fixed! If our hearts are broken because of a guy or a girl, they can be fixed. If our families are broken, they can be fixed. (And, if by chance, our parents do get divorced, let us fix our own selves and learn from them so we won't give our children a broken home.) If we're bad in English, science, history, or math, it can be fixed. If we're slow runners, bad jumpers, poor musicians, lousy dancers, terrible drivers, fat, skinny, or just plain ugly, we can be fixed! You don't throw a twenty-thousand-dollar car away just because a fifteen-dollar part doesn't work! People are the same way! That's why we can never say never. That's why we must act now and commit to fix what is broken. If we don't, we will surely slide down into a lax state of complacency, perhaps never to recover. If you think about it, the slide has already begun which will not only ruin us but our future children.

We're much different from our parents and it isn't all good. We're getting lazy! My father had three jobs, raised four kids, and went to night school. If I go to the cleaners and 7-Eleven in the same day, I need a nap!

My dad could fix anything, but I've had a VCR for five years and it's still flashing midnight!

Is it possible that our children will be lazier than we are? Think about that for a few days! I can hear us lecturing our kids, saying, "I didn't have my own American Express card like you when I was your age. When I needed money, I actually had to go to my father and ask for it! And it was darn hard, stressful work. One time I had to cry fifteen minutes before he gave me all I asked for!

Yes, "STUFF HAPPENS"—to teenagers, to adults, to us, and eventually to our children. So, what are we going to do about it? Hopefully we won't quit like many do but will strive to better understand the necessity for obstacles in our lives. Let me explain.

I believe in rainbows. They are beautiful and the very sight of one brightens our day. We find our "pots of gold" at the end of a rainbow. We see a rainbow as nature's message that the best is yet to be.

I also believe in storms. You've got to have a storm in order to have a rainbow!

I've had some tough times in my life, just as you have— we've all experienced stormy weather. We've all had obstacles and resistance that we've had to deal with and overcome. But that's part of life's deal!

You don't take the water out of the swimming pool to make it easier to swim to the other side. Sure, the water offers resistance, but that's why we take swimming lessons and learn the different strokes. As we effectively swim and deal with the resistance of the water, we propel ourselves through the water to our desired destination.

Resistance and obstacles should not be removed from our lives! Facing them head-on helps us grow stronger and improve!

From a football player's perspective, it's absolutely no fun to run across an empty field. Anybody can do that! Where the fun and excitement and challenge come in is when there are eleven guys out there on the opposing team trying to tackle you and knock you out. Now you have to prove what you're made of. Now you have to put on a few moves, get up when you're down, and rearrange your face each and every time your helmet is knocked sideways and you're looking out your earhole!

Let's face it, because life presents stormy weather, let us commit right now to WEATHERING THE STORM!

Yes, "stuff" happens, and we must weather the storm! To assist you I have written this book.

This is not a book on Motivation. Most people think Inspiration and Motivation mean the same. They do not! Inspiration affects attitude—the way we think. Motivation affects behavior—the way we act. Therefore, no one can motivate another. We can't get anyone to do anything unless they themselves choose to do it. All we can hope to do is inspire one another to want to motivate ourselves. Change and improvement must come from within! To be a champion athlete, it's what we do when the coach is not around that makes us a champion. The coach can't motivate players. He can only inspire us to become the best we can be. We aren't running for the coach—we're running because we want to be champions. To be a champion student, it's what we do when the teacher is not around that makes us a champion. We're not doing our homework to please our teachers or parents—we're studying because they inspire us to understand why we should.

Alcoholics Anonymous verifies the value of Inspiration in a slogan, "You can't carry the alcoholic. You can only carry the message. You can't go into the bar and drag out the drunk. You can only inspire him by example and call to him to come out on his own. AA is a program of Attraction—not Promotion!"

This is an Inspirational book!

This is not a book on Peer Pressure!

"Peer pressure" is an overused catch-all phrase that is everyone's excuse for bad, inexcusable, negative behavior.

"Pressure" is not something that is naturally there. It's created when you question your own ability. When you know what you can do, there is never any question! And the way you find out what you can do is through spaced repetition practice. The time to learn to say no to negative influences like tobacco, alcohol and drugs is not when you're surrounded by people doing them. It is when you're free of negative emotional influence.

Practice develops confidence and eliminates the outside pressure of others. In fact, practice creates inside pressure called desire. Pressure is negative—Desire is positive! Desire comes as we discover who we are and what we want to become. The more desire we develop, the stronger we are and the easier it becomes to withstand the negative insecure influences of others. Desire pushes us to "walk on higher ground" and find friends who accept us as we are.

When you have desire, you simply hang around with people who share your same value system (a code of behavior that defines what is appropriate.) These kinds of people accept you for who you are, not for what you look like. They don't expect you to change your hairstyles, health habits, and moral standards to please them. They won't put "pressure" on you to do something that you don't want to do. Yes, dealing with so-called "Peer Pressure" is simple if you want it to be. If you hang around with people who don't smoke, they won't put "pressure" on you to smoke. If you hang around with people who don't drink alcohol or do drugs, they won't put "pressure" on you to get drunk or get stoned.

If you hang around with girls or boys who have the same high moral standards that you have, people who understand that love is a commitment—not a way of feeling, who dress modestly because they understand that if it's not for sale—don't put it on the menu, they won't put "pressure" on you to have sex.

Remember, people are influenced either from without or from within. It's your choice. You're in charge! Pressure is not something that is naturally there. It is created when you question your own ability. So hang around with people who are good, clean, pure, positive influences on developing your ability. Only feel pressure from within and develop this burning desire to become the very best you can possibly be! Then, simply be true to you!

This is a Desire book!

This is not a book on Time Management.

Managing your time really means managing your behavior. Time discriminates against no one. We all get 24 hours a day—168 hours per week. Time is constant for everyone. It does not change! Therefore, to change what is happening, the only thing we can do is change what we are doing—change our habits—take charge and control the events in our day. It is odd when someone says, "I don't have time." We have all the time there is! Let us manage it by managing ourselves:

Manage our "plans and purpose." Have a specific mission to accomplish.

Manage our "parasites." The time wasters called T.V., phone calls, waiting for buses, and arguing with family and friends.

Manage our "procrastinations." Simply do what's right when you're supposed to do it. Learn to do unpleasant things before pleasurable ones. Like our mothers told us, "Eat your spinach first, then your dessert."

This is a book on personal behavior management!

This is not a book on Goal Setting. Goal Setting has been way overdone. In fact, it has been way misunderstood! Goals are only an excuse for the game. We play the game in between the goals. We need to put the emphasis on enjoying the practice process of the journey and not put so much emphasis on the destination. "It's not the sugar that makes the tea sweet—it's the stirring—it's the process."

Goals don't provide positive attitude and motivation; playing the game does! This is a book about achieving and enjoying daily successes and how to love playing the game of life. Let me explain.

Most athletes get satisfaction only from playing the game at game time, yet they practice two hours each day—four days a week. That equals eight hours of practice time and thirty minutes of playing time each week. No wonder they don't produce during practice and run only when the coach is watching! Not a happiness-reaping arrangement, to say the least! We must, therefore, learn to enjoy the daily grind if lasting happiness and true success is what we seek. I remember playing little league baseball, looking through the fence, dreaming about the day I could wear a high school uniform. When that day came and I got the uniform, it was no big deal. In high school, I dreamed about the day when I could wear a college uniform. And when that day came, the uniform was no big deal. You see, we must find satisfaction in the simple, daily routine of the practice and the grind.

If you want an A on a test, a paper, or in a class, say that is what you want and then forget about it. Then, if you simply do your homework tonight to the very best of your ability, and when the next night comes, you do your homework to the very best of your ability, and when the next night comes you do your homework to the very best of your ability, the A on the test, on the paper, and in the class will take care of themselves! Sure, it is fun and important to focus your efforts on the long-term goal— the end result, but you must use it only for direction. When you take care of *now,* you eliminate the worry, and the future takes care of itself. When you engage in daily positive action, you are going to do what you need to do *right now* to make yourself successful.

This is a playbook of strategies for positive daily living. It teaches us that when we know the end result is a definite bargain, we will willingly pay the price today so we can enjoy what it buys forever. This is a book that reminds us that the best way to predict the future is to create it!

This is not a book on friendship or relationships. To have a friend you must first be a friend. We need to become the best we can be first before we can help others.

On an airplane there is always a preflight safety demonstration, part of which runs, "In case of a loss in cabin pressure, an oxygen mask will appear. Place it over your nose and mouth, securing it tightly." Then it goes on to say, "If you are traveling with a small child, take care of your own oxygen mask first. Only then will you be strong enough to assist the child with his or her needs."

If we don't take care of our own needs first and foremost, we will eventually miss out on many opportunities that would make us truly happy. If we're always trying to please others, we will end up hanging around with people who are selfish and who don't have our interests at heart. Ask yourself if you are hanging around with friends who are literally taking your wishes and dreams away because they are too caught up in their own personal problems? See if you can relate to this story.

Three survivors of a shipwreck had been marooned on an island for two years, surviving only on coconuts and fruit. One day a bottle washed up on the shore. One of the men pulled out its cork and a genie emerged. "Thank you for freeing me," said the genie. "I now must grant each of you one wish."

The first man said, "I wish I were in Hawaii surrounded by beautiful women and the finest food; retired and care-free." In a flash his wish was granted and he disappeared.

The second man said, "I wish to have ten million dollars in the bank so I'll be set up to buy anything I ever wanted." Again there was a flash, and the second man disappeared.

The genie turned to the third man, "And you?" he asked.

The third man looked glum, self-centered, and depressed. "I don't know," he said. "I'm lonesome and miserable. I wish those guys were back here!"

What kind of a friend are you? Do you build people up or bring them down to your level? Before any of us can be a true friend and unselfishly give of ourselves in a relationship, we must first like and love ourselves.

This is a self-help, liking-and-loving-yourself book!

This is not a book on building self-esteem. Self-esteem is overrated! When we have high self-esteem, we think well of ourselves. That's it. Period. You may say, So what? Big deal. I know many people who feel good about themselves but never accomplish anything! Sure they try things and go through the motions, but they never try very hard. They never give it their very best and endure to the end. They start many things and finish very few. What good then is a sense of high self-esteem? I even know people with high self-esteem who do drugs.

For this reason, let us introduce a different phrase—a more appropriate phrase that must precede building self-esteem. This phrase is *self-effectiveness*. Effectiveness means *doing things right*. Only when we do the right things can we develop and sustain high self-esteem! A high sense of self-effectiveness simply means that we have a strong belief that we *can accomplish;* that we can affect the world by our own actions, we can and will make our dreams come true. Self-effectiveness is a deep conviction that it is better and easier to act our way into positive thinking than to think our way into positive action. It is a deep conviction (based on experience) that we can and will work hard enough to accomplish—not later on, but right now!

Dr. Wendy Ritchua, a psychologist, feels that it is vitally important to understand this distinction between esteem and effectiveness. "Parents are told to build up their child's self-esteem. But that is such a nebulous concept. Parents don't always know how to go about it. Helping someone to *do* something is a lot easier than helping him or her to achieve some overall feeling. And being successful at *doing* is really what establishes self-esteem."

Ask yourself: What makes successful peak performers give their very best? What makes them successful? Where does this motivation come from? The answer lies in focusing on a *vision*. Vision creates purpose and provides a self-identified, self-important reason to succeed.

Picture a musician absorbed in learning a new piece of

music, a student thoroughly involved in a scientific experiment, an athlete excited about becoming stronger in the weight room. What keeps these individuals motivated, involved, and, most important, committed to the end is their love of the activity and their belief in the vision of what they will accomplish.

Successful peak performers have discovered that their goals can actually be achieved. Everyone has dreams and ideas, but successful peak performers extend themselves to put those ideas into practice. It may take an exceptional effort to achieve a goal, but successful peak performers always endure because they believe in their vision. They know that every time they turn a dream or idea (a vision) into reality, they learn and believe and, best of all, remember that they can do it again. Then, they *do* just that! Again and again. They understand that the only difference between successful people and unsuccessful people is that successful peak performers do what unsuccessful people will not do. And successful people don't want to do it either—but they do it anyway! They know that in order to achieve their goals and become the very best they can possibly be, they must do *what* needs to be done *when* it needs to be done!

This is a self-effectiveness book—a book on hard work, perseverance, and doing the right things now!

This is not a book about drug abuse or "Just Saying No." How trite! We have to take it one step further and do more than that. We must *decide to say no!* It's better and easier to build a fence at the edge of the cliff than to park an ambulance at its base. Therefore, we can't just talk the talk—we must walk the walk. We must get out of the planning stage and into the go stage of positive actions. We can't just say no, we must *do no!* Let me explain.

There are only twenty-four hours in a day. We can't be at two places at the same time. We cannot do two things at once. So, instead of worrying so much about how to say no to alcohol and drugs, if we simply say yes to something positive, we won't have time to do something negative, and our positive actions will say no for us!

I'm sick and tired of ex-druggies standing up and telling about their wild escapades and concluding their speeches with "Just say no!" I think, "Like you did?" This sounds like a harmful message that tells you that you can go ahead and sow some wild oats and change later. This is irresponsible behavior on the part of these meeting planners and speakers!

If by chance you have already experimented with drugs, it is time to stop, learn from your mistakes, forgive yourself and others, and move ahead. Remember that failure is an event, not a person. No matter what your past has been, you have a spotless future. Today is the first day of the rest of your life! Let's not live in the past and glamorize it. We all have a past. We've all made some big mistakes. Let's not make a big deal out of it! Let us live for today and plan a new exciting future filled with successful ???????

This is a just-say-yes-to-life book! And, yes, I realize saying yes to life is often difficult, but that's part of the deal. Setbacks, heartbreak, obstacles, trials, and tribulations are all part of the reality of life.

Let's face it: sometimes it's just plain tough—too tough!! And suicide is not the answer. Suicide is a permanent solution to a temporary problem! You have to deal with life while you're alive, but you also have to deal with death when you're dead!! Time heals all. Suicide is nowhere near an alternative solution. If you think about killing yourself, you are not crazy. Just get some professional help and get on with your life. School is tough; relationships are tough; life is tough—Yes—but if you're not failing a few times, it means you're not pushing yourself hard enough! So, what it boils down to is *perspective:* how you look at it. You can't always choose the situation you're in, but you can always choose whether or not to smile. Ask yourself, What is my perspective?

Do you sometimes feel like a sea animal living on land, wanting to fly in the air? If so, these frustrations are no big deal! Just remember we are in charge of our lives and our destinies, so we can change! And the best way to change is to develop proper perspective and condition ourselves to always keep the big picture in mind. Ask yourself: Where am I coming from? Where have I been? Where am I going? How do I see and perceive life?

What about perspective as it pertains to *now* and *then:* The chief cause of failure in life is giving up what we want most for what we want at the moment.

Do we keep our lives with their trials and tribulations in proper perspective? Have you talked for a few hours with a teenager who has cerebral palsy? Have you ever visited a classroom of young people in special education, physically and mentally challenged young people? Have you ever watched or participated in a Special Olympics competition? Have you ever spent time with a little boy who is dying of a terminal illness? Or spent time with a little girl who loves to watch dancers but yet has no legs? What is your perspective? Do you feel picked on and pathetic? Do you think that you have problems that cannot be solved? While some people are worried about clothes, boys, girls, dates, and cars, others are just trying to walk or live one more day.

What is your perspective? How do you see your life and the part you play in it? Are you really fortunate or are you really deprived? How and on what are you spending your time? If you had only one day to live how would you be acting differently? What would you be doing with your time? What matters most to you?

What Matters Most

Answer the following series of questions.

I have a steel I-beam that is 120 feet long (they are used in constructing bridges and large buildings). The beam is on the floor; it is solid and secure. You are standing on one end of the beam, and I am standing on the other end of the beam with a $50 bill. Will you walk across the 120-foot long steel beam without touching the floor to get the $50? I will assume you answered yes.

I have now taken the steel I-beam to New York City. A crane has lifted it to the top of the World Trade Center. The World Trade Center has the two tallest twin towers in the world; they are 1,360 feet high. The beam has been positioned to span the distance between the two twin towers so that one end is resting on the roof of one tower and the other end is resting on the roof of the other tower. Again, the twin towers are 1,360 feet straight up (or straight down, depending on which end you are on!).

You are on one roof standing on one end of the beam; I am standing on the other roof at the other end of the steel beam with a $50 bill. It is raining, and the wind is blowing. Will you now walk across the I-beam (without touching the floor) to get the $50 bill? No? How about for $100? No, again? How about for $1,000,000? (If you fall off, you won't get the money!) No, again? Will you walk across the I-beam for $10,000,000? No, no, no?

Let's change the circumstances. A lunatic kidnapper has just abducted your son or daughter or little brother or sister. He sends word to you, standing on one roof, that unless you walk across that 120 foot I-beam to save your loved one, the kidnapper will drop your loved one to his or her death. Will you now go across? Yes? Good! I would, too. I think everyone that I know would now walk across the beam!

What we have done here is identify *what matters most.* When the I-beam was on the floor, we would willingly walk across for $50; therefore, money matters most!

When the I-beam was taken to the top of the World Trade Center's twin towers to span the two towers at 1,360 feet high in the air, we identified that safety matters most.

We would not walk across for any amount of money—safety matters most!

But when the kidnapper put our loved one on the line, we discovered that more important to us than money, more important to us than safety, is the love we have for this person. Consequently, this love and commitment to family stands out as one of the governing values in our lives. And notice something: How long did we have to take to decide to walk across the beam to save the child? Not long at all! When we take the necessary time to focus on *what matters most,* our behavior immediately follows as a natural consequence. When we focus on *what matters most,* our perspective immediately stays in check and balance, and our motivation for living life to its fullest remains constant and secure.

Again, what is your present perspective on life and love? Are you spending your time on positive, productive things? Remember, never once has an armored truck followed a hearse to the cemetery. You can't take it with you! Have you identified all the people, places, and things that matter most to you? When we do, it doesn't matter what happens, we can and will deal with it!

Because "stuff" always happens to children and young adults, let us take a moment here to reflect on some of the crucial issues and philosophical behavior measurements that "matter most" to you. Evaluate your present philosophies and teaching techniques that you adhere to and see if you are helping or hurting young people or your fellow peers in their struggle to identify and follow through on "what matters most."

Because a lot of parents aren't being parents anymore (it doesn't make sense to bring a child into the world if parents won't take the time to show it to them), the following pleas from "straight" kids as well as "wild" kids who are seriously in trouble with the law truly help us focus on the most important principles and parenting skills we need to believe in. See if you agree with this national survey.

A WHAT-MATTERS-MOST MEMO
FROM A CHILD TO HIS PARENTS

1. Don't spoil me. I know quite well that I ought not to have all that I ask for—I'm only testing you.
2. Don't be afraid to be firm with me and set curfews and rules. I prefer it. It makes me feel secure.
3. Don't protect me from consequences. Sometimes I need to learn the painful way.
4. Don't let me form bad habits. I have to rely on you to detect them in the early stages and give me direction by example.
5. Don't make me feel smaller than I am. It only makes me behave stupidly and prove that I am "big."
6. Don't correct me in front of people if you can help it. Praise in public; chastise in private.
7. Don't make me feel that my mistakes are sins. It upsets my sense of values.
8. Don't put me off when I ask questions. If you do, you will find that I'll stop asking you and seek information elsewhere.
9. Don't tell me my fears are silly. They are real to me and you can do much to reassure me if you try to understand.
10. Don't ever suggest that you are perfect or infallible. It hurts and disappoints me when I learn you are neither.
11. Don't be inconsistent. That confuses me and makes me lose faith in you.
12. Don't ever think that it is beneath your dignity to apologize to me. An honest apology makes me feel surprisingly warm toward you.
13. Don't forget that I can't thrive without lots of love and understanding. I need your quantity and quality time and your affection.
14. Please keep yourself fit and healthy. I need you and I

love you. Please don't die early because you smoke, drink too much, or use drugs.

15. Because "stuff happens," let's stick together. I believe in you. I need you and hope you believe in me.

Yes "stuff" does happen. And according to the bumper sticker, "stuff" may even exude a slight odor.

One day I was speaking at a school in Columbus, Ohio, when a young handicapped boy caught my eye as he sat in the corner hallway. His name was Stuart Lewis and, although he was *in* school, a private tutor was teaching him all the standard subjects. The unique thing about him was that Stu has never, ever, spoken a word. He couldn't move his legs, arms, head, or mouth. He was strapped to a wheel chair and communicated only through a plexiglass window, labeled with the alphabet letters lined in columns, with the numbers one through zero arranged across the top. Stu sat in his wheel chair on one side of the plexiglass window and looked at each letter to spell out each word in each sentence of every thought he had. His tutor sat on the other side of the plexiglass and watched Stu's eyes as he looked at each letter or number. She would then speak each letter or number and literally spell out each word that Stu communicated. As one can imagine, it often took several minutes just to communicate one thought; just to communicate one sentence. Yet remarkably, Stu was comfortably in the ninth grade doing standard ninth-grade work, passing standard ninth-grade tests with the rest of his ninth-grade friends. In fact, Stu is above average—a brilliant 4.0 student!

I found something else out about Stu. I had the privilege to spend an hour with him talking back and forth, using his glass communication board. He had a great sense of humor, loved heavy-metal music (his idol was Gene Simmons), wanted desperately to make a living one day as a television series comedy writer, and interestingly enough deeply understood the bumper sticker " 'stuff' happens."

Because Stu couldn't write, I recently received a letter from his father that explains Stu's interpretation of "stuff happens." Here is an excerpt from the letter that capsulizes Stu's feelings and inspires us to weather the storm. "Stuart once told me, after seeing a blind person, how unfortunate the blind person must be since he had lost his sight and couldn't enjoy seeing the world around him. I asked Stu if he felt that he too had a handicap that prevented him from enjoying many aspects of 'normal life,' such as walking or using his hands. Stuart said that he was born that way and that was normal for him."

Stuart's actions are simply "normal" for him. What is "normal" for you? And . . . are you striving to be better than normal? If not, why not? As we strive for perfection, most of us never reach perfection. But, in the process we attain excellence and become much more than we thought we could be!

This brings us to the most important question so far: Are you the very best you can possibly be right now, or can you and will you become better?

To assist you in your quest for excellence and personal best, you must understand *practical application.* We need to realize that good can always come from bad—that lemons can be turned into lemonade if we will simply take the time to figure out how to apply what we know to what is happening to us.

For example, I remember getting my first kiss (back in college!) and trying to figure out the technique to getting another one! At that time in my life I was an athlete, and I couldn't figure out how going to math class could possibly help me become a professional football player. Then one day it dawned on me: Mathematics is important. In fact, the sooner I learned math, the sooner I could start applying it to my everyday life to help all of my dreams come true—including getting this next kiss which was so important to me. The following poem describes exactly what happened as I used mathematics to accomplish my goal. (I'm sure most guys can relate to this!)

Practical Application

He's teaching her arithmetic, he said it was his mission;
He kissed her once, he kissed her twice, and said, "Now that's addition."
And as he added smack by smack in silent satisfaction,
She sweetly gave the kisses back and said, "Now that's subtraction."
Then he kissed her, she kissed him without an explanation.
Then both together smiled and said, "That's multiplication."
The Dad appeared upon the scene and made a quick decision,
He kicked that kid three blocks away and said, "That's long division."

When we fully understand *practical application*—that no matter what happens, we can learn and grow from it and apply it positively to our lives, we automatically move to a higher level and accept another principle of success: *understanding*. Let us understand understanding.

A store owner was tacking a sign above his store door that read "Puppies for Sale." Signs like that have a way of attracting small children, and, sure enough, a little boy appeared under the store owner's sign. "How much are you going to sell the puppies for?" he asked.

The store owner replied, "Anywhere from $30 to $50."

The little boy reached in his pocket and pulled out some change. "I have $2.37," he said. "Can I please look at them?"

The store owner smiled and whistled and out of the kennel came Lady, who ran down the aisle of his store followed by five little, teeny, tiny balls of fur. One puppy was lagging considerably behind. Immediately the little boy singled out the lagging, limping puppy and said, "What's wrong with that little dog?"

The store owner explained that the veterinarian had examined the little dog and had discovered that it didn't have a hip socket. It would always limp. It would always be lame. The little boy became excited. "That is the little puppy I want to buy."

The store owner said "No, you don't want to buy that little dog. If you really want him, I'll just give him to you."

The little boy got ticked off. He looked straight in the store owner's eyes, pointing his finger, and said, "I don't want you to give him to me. That little dog is worth every bit as much as all the other dogs and I'll pay full price. In fact, I'll give you $2.37 now, and 50 cents a month until I have him paid for."

The store owner countered, "You really don't want to buy this little dog. He is never going to be able to run and jump and play with you like the other puppies."

To this, the little boy reached down and rolled up his pant leg to reveal a badly twisted, crippled left leg supported by a big metal brace. He looked up at the store owner and softly replied, "Well, I don't run so well myself, and the little puppy will need someone who understands!"

Understanding ourselves (not letting what we cannot do interfere with what we can do) and understanding friends, school, family, and the purpose of life is a fundamental key to *success*. In fact, understanding is fundamental to *weathering the storm*. Understanding breeds patience to endure the bad weather until the good finally comes.

Patient as a Snail

One raw, rainy, windy day a snail started to climb a cherry tree. Some birds in a neighboring tree chattered their ridicule. "Hey, you dumb snail. Where do you think you are going?" said one of them. "Why are you climbing that tree? There are no cherries on it."

"There will be when I get there," said the snail.

Ask yourself, Are you patient, understanding, and climbing higher by working hard with a positive perspective toward accomplishing your goal? If not, why not? Don't settle for mediocrity! Take a stand! Change! You can be the person you dream to be!! Just find someone you can idolize and look up to. Then, simply duplicate what they are doing. Acting like a champion is the only way to become a champion! Just find a positive role model and follow his or her actions and advice!

Role Models

Before we can ever hope and believe that we can accomplish our goals and become the person we dream about, we must first believe that it is possible to do what we dream about. This belief comes in the form of a positive *role model.*

Positive role models are successful people we admire and emulate. They are the evidence that we can change and succeed.

Studies of successful peak performers indicate that they always have role models who have made an exemplary effort toward their own personal goals. Role models, then, are "permission statements" that clearly state: *If someone else can do it and become it, what one can do I can do, too. If I simply work hard, commit myself to the end, and duplicate what these successful peak performers have done, I can and will be successful!*

Role models are real heroes who live by high values and ethical standards of performance. They are not to be confused with celebrities who are famous only because of publicity. True heroes and real role models are identified by positive deeds and exemplary living.

I lucked out. I didn't have to go looking for role models; I had heroes in my very own house. My mother and my father have never let me down. Confused me, maybe, but never let me down. They always taught me correct principles and showed me the way. In fact, this book came about because of one of my parent's continuing encouraging-word phrases. At least once a day, each and every day of my life, my mother and father tell me "Dan, we become what we think about. So go for it! When you lose your dreams, you die. You were born to succeed!"

The first part of the statement always bothers me. "We become what we think about." It's not true! If it was true, I would have been a woman by the time I was twelve years old!

How about the second part of this motherly/fatherly advice: "So go for it! When you lose your dreams, you die." I suppose it is true. That is why we have so many people walking around our world right now who are dead, and they don't even know it yet. They've stopped dreaming dreams. They have become content and, therefore, they're dead. They are not living—they are merely existing, vegetating, surviving.

How about the last part of this statement? "You were born to succeed." Now this is the part that really gets to me. I acknowledge it is simple, but it really bothers me. Just maybe it doesn't apply to everyone. Especially not to me! It doesn't seem fair that I fail more than my share of the time. (When I go golfing, I lose balls in the ball washer! The other day, my dog got hit by a bus—twice! In the same day!! As a sophomore in high school, I had so many pimples that when I fell asleep in my math class, the kids played connect-the-dots on my face! When I was in the third grade, I almost died of cancer. Over a seventeen-year period of time, I've broken my neck, back, nose, jaw, both hands, both thumbs, both little fingers. I've had my head sewn up eleven times, have had two hernias, an emergency appendectomy, blown out both knees three times each, and have blown out both ankles twice. And, yes, I've also been fired from a job and have had girls break my heart and drop me cold on my you-know-what! I don't know about you, but, frankly, I'm just happy to be here!)

However, regardless of the trials, tribulations, or the

number of times that I have fallen, through it all, to this day, my parents still say, "Dan, you were born to succeed!!"

My parents have also suffered and sacrificed much in their lives. They, too, have experienced many disappointments along their way. So, why are they continually optimistic about everything? Do they have brain damage? Has their butter plum slipped off their biscuits? Where did this positive attitude and action outlook born-to-succeed philosophy come from?

The only thing I can come up with is that it started when my Grandfather Clark decided to visit the South Sea Islands as a young man. He spent many years there living and learning from the old chiefs and wise men. He became dear friends with the natives and locals who were direct descendants from ancient Hawaiian kings. After his sacred and unique schooling, he finally returned to the main land, arriving with a large chest full of secret things he'd acquired.

My grandfather soon got married and became an outstanding master teacher (he taught school until the day he died). He also traveled around the country making speeches to schools, educators, and executives. In his spare time, he successfully raised eight children (including my dad), became a very successful father and spiritual, community leader. He died of a heart attack when he was ninety-three years old. He was a very wise, distinguished man, who gave so much to his family and friends, that he literally wore himself out. His heart never failed to beat for others, and finally it came to a stop when his service was done.

I don't remember much about my grandfather except that he always told everyone, "You were born to succeed." When asked what it meant, he would always point to three wooden signs he had hanging up on his wall in his home. He had made these signs himself. One was simply five letters engraved in the middle of a board. No one ever knew what those five letters meant, but they inspired him greatly. For each time he saw them, a smile came to his face and he seemed to increase the amount of time he spent with others. The sign read: WGACA.

Grandfather's second sign always made people stop and think. It was a deep, philosophical poem put in a simple catchy way that reads like a rap! When he made this sign, I suppose Grandfather wanted to get us to think not with our minds, but with our consciences. He never explained the sign's meaning to anybody, so I won't attempt it either. Ponder the poem and take time to interpret its message before you go on. The second sign read:

> You are the message, so how are they reacting,
> It's not the length of your play, but the quality of acting.
> Are you real and right and authentically you,
> Do you do what you say and say what you do?
> If you don't win, does the winner break the record?
> 'Cause you're pushin' each other toward the checkered.
> Do you scratch where it itches and improve each day?
> Do you fix what is broken along your way?
> Have you worked so you're needed for what you do?
> Are you leaving this world in better shape when you're through?
> If so—I like me best when I'm with you!

Grandfather's third wooden sign was his favorite. It not only inspired him the way the other signs did, but it filled him and our family with pride. Grandfather was very proud and honored to be a school teacher, and this simple sign always reminded him of why it was worth it to him to put up with poor pay to be a professional professor. This wooden sign read:

> Teaching Is the Profession
> That Makes All Other Professions Possible

Whenever Grandfather got discouraged or challenged about his chosen profession as a teacher, whenever he felt as though he wasn't making a positive difference in our world, he always reflected on his favorite parable.

A king sent word out throughout the land that he wanted to honor the greatest subjects in his kingdom. The day finally came to pay tribute to these outstar. ling leaders for their achievements. The first subject was brought before him. The king asked his servant, "What has this man done for the kingdom?"

The servant replied, "This man is a well-respected physician. A doctor who has healed the sick and helped save our people."

The second subject was brought before him. The king asked, "What has she done for the kingdom?"

The servant replied, "She is an architect. She is well-respected, the designer of most of the large buildings in our country. She has lent beauty to our cities and has built our places of commerce."

The third subject was brought before the king. The king asked, "What has this woman done for the kingdom?"

The servant replied, "This woman is an accountant—the keeper of our books. Her careful calculations have kept our kingdom thriving and prosperous."

Finally, an old, silver-haired, wrinkled man was brought before the king. The king sarcastically asked his servant, "What can this old man have possibly done for the kingdom?"

The servant replied, "I have presented you with a physician, an architect, and with an accountant. This man was their teacher!"

The king came down off his throne to gratefully pay proper tribute and respect to this man who had given so much to the world!

It's true. Teaching is the profession that makes all other professions possible!

Telling this parable always ignited the orator in Grandfather as he concluded by sharing his opinion about "true education."

True Education

Dr. Stephen E. Cosgrove said, "The essence of education is to provide an opportunity to create options for ourselves and others. The more we know, the more we can do with what we know!"

The trend of "back to the basics" must consist of more than reading, writing, and arithmetic. Learning this in a sterile environment makes no sense. Our society is much different now, and, therefore, we must educate the total person. For this reason, I am a big fan of vocational education. I have taught that this is the focal point in education where one could take reading, writing, and arithmetic and apply it to everyday, practical living. Instead of preaching, "Keep the best and shoot the rest!" and catering only to the 25 percent of high-school students who go on to college, we must realize that *true education* is "applied knowledge," which effects everyone! Let us always remember that continued education and advanced training is a must in everyone's life, but a four-year college degree is not necessarily the answer for everyone! Society needs supertalented, master mechanics, plumbers, police officers, cabinetmakers, and electronics engineers, as well as doctors, lawyers, and corporate presidents. I have always challenged my fellow teachers to develop a good personal relationship with their B and C students, because they are the ones who will eventually become the successful small-business backbone of their communities. *A* students usually became the teachers."

Oh, how Grandfather loved being a teacher!

Yes, teaching truly is the profession that makes all other professions possible. Teachers should be and always will be the most honored and respected individuals in any community, even though their paychecks don't reflect it (someday they will). Teaching is the most noble profession in the world. Grandfather definitely had a reason to be proud. In fact, he was more than proud. He was obsessed with being the very best teacher he could possibly be. He understood that he was a teacher not only while he was in the classroom, but that teaching was a 100 percent, twenty-four-hour-a-day commitment to excellence, not just through the spoken word, but through personal exemplary action. Grandfather had a burning desire and obvious passion to leave people, places, and things in better shape than he had found them. He was deeply committed to teaching more than curriculum—he taught students! He believed he was in the people-building business! Grandfather loved to teach and talk about education.

Now Grandfather has passed away and is buried and gone and no one has seen the chest since. But life goes on, and we will always remember his three signs and his constant encouraging words to my father, which have been passed down to me: "You were born to succeed." And I suppose I will also pass it along to my children, because "stuff" happens to everyone in every generation. Every person in every generation will have to weather the storm. And I suppose they will pass along the same information to their children.

Life does go on and on as new births continue to verify it. And, yes, each baby truly is born to succeed. The question, then, is, If everyone is born to succeed, why then do so many fail? Why do so many flake out along the way? Everyone is born positive with the dream to succeed but most die negative and content with mediocrity. Why? What can be done to ensure success? What and where are the answers? Is there something they are not teaching us in school? Everyone who knew him, know Grandfather had *all* the answers. If only Grandfather had left his answers. . . .

It was a cold, rainy day and it took all I had to weather the storm. I'm an outdoor man and hate to be cooped up inside—especially in the country. I had come to visit my grandmother and was planning to stay here for the whole summer. She lived in an old house north of Los Angeles with a big backyard set against a backdrop of mountains. Sure, I was a teenager, but I still loved hiking and exploring the territory around her home. Sometimes I even fantasized about being a great explorer and discovering a lost treasure. I knew it would never happen to me, but the thought was sure amusing! Amusing until a day like today.

Today the weather was so brutal, I was forced to find something to do in the house. Luckily, Grandmother had a huge house with plenty of places to explore. One such place was the attic. I climbed up the rickety stairs and peered in. It was big and dark and damp. Today it was also spooky because of the rain. Each time the thunder rumbled, the house shook and the dim lights flickered off and on. After one particular loud crackle and boom, I got so spooked that I decided to go back downstairs. As I was climbing down the ladder, I glanced up to notice a funny-looking piece of wood protruding out of an old chest. I climbed back up the ladder and opened the lid.

The chest belonged to my grandfather. His name was stenciled on the top. My grandfather had died a few years before and his chest had not been seen or opened up since. Cobwebs were everywhere except on the strange-looking piece of wood that had originally caught my eye. I pulled the piece of wood out of the chest to examine it more closely. It was shiny and didn't have a scratch on it. I could tell it was very old, but it looked brand new. On one side of it there was an engraved inscription in fancy cursive, old-world English script that read WGACA. Wow! I remember seeing these same letters on the wooden sign on Grandfather's wall in his home! I wondered what the letters meant until I found the small wood-covered book that had the same letters engraved on it. I brushed back the dust and immediately opened the book to see what it contained. As I read, to my pleasant surprise, I found that the book was a brief autobiography of my grandfather.

Grandfather passed away when I was a young man, so I didn't get to know him very well. Consequently, this book was a gold mine to me and promised to help answer many questions about Grandfather and what made him tick. Even though it was only twelve pages, it was written by my grandfather in his own handwriting and seemed to be full of interesting facts and philosophies of life. Surprisingly, this book was the only thing in the big chest that had interested our entire family for so many years. Everyone wondered what was in the chest that Grandfather so frequently opened up for inspiration and guidance. Now I was going to find out!

I eagerly opened the wood-covered book. The twelve pages represented twelve sacred, philosophical challenges. I now quote Grandfather, and pass along the following sacred solutions to one and all.

CHALLENGE 1

WGACA

The strange-looking, odd-shaped piece of wood accompanying this sacred book is made from monkeypot, a wood native to the South Sea Islands. It is called a boomerang. This boomerang is an ancient object given to me by Chief Lani O Puoo. Used as a reusable weapon when thrown out, it returns to the thrower. He who sends—receives. It symbolizes what the true successful life cycle is all about. It is engraved, as is the cover of this book, with five letters: WGACA. This philosophic acronym stands for *What Goes Around, Comes Around.* It is appropriate that it is engraved deep in the side of this boomerang, for it definitely goes around and comes around.

Let "WGACA" be known here, and now, and forever, as the *boomerang theory.* If you take care of the air, the air will take care of you. If you take care of the water, the water will take care of you. If you take care of the land, the land will take care of you. If you take care of people, people will take care of you. If you build up others, they will build up you. If you serve others, others will serve you. But if you hurt others, others will also hurt you.

Positive or negative—WGACA—What goes around, comes around!

This boomerang theory has been passed on through the ages in many forms and has even taken the ancient measurement form called the *golden rule*. All of the great religions have their own versions.

Golden Rules of the Great Religions

"True rule is to guard and do by the things of others, as you do by your own" (the Hindus from the Veda; the Brahmans, the Upenishads).

"One should seek for others the happiness one desires for oneself" (the Buddhists from the Tripitaka).

"Do as you would be done by" (the Zoroastrians from the Zend-Avesta).

"What you do not wish done to yourself, do not to others" (the Confucians from the Analects).

"Let none of you treat your brother in a way he himself would dislike to be treated" (the Mohammedans from the Koran).

"Whatsoever you do not wish your neighbor to do you, do not unto him" (the Jews from the Torah).

"All things whatsoever ye would that men should do to you, do ye even so to them" (the Christians from the Bible).

All of these are important—all have the same message. But each of these is still too aloof for me. I'm surprised someone didn't just write, "What goes around, comes around." Therefore, let me explain it this way: Take two children and put a piece of cake in front of them. If you have one child cut the cake to allow them to share, and you let the other child take first choice of the two pieces, it is amazing how precise and evenly the cake is cut and divided. Can you see the importance of doing unto others as you would have them do unto you? If so, it is time to introduce my golden rules. I realize they are simple, but it is the simple list that floats my boat. They prove true, the ten two-little-word statements: "If it is to be, it is up to me." And take us one step higher to the understanding that "what goes around, comes around" doesn't just work with others, it also works when dealing with ourselves.

The title of this little list is My Golden Rules.

If you open it, close it. (Brilliant, eh?)
If you turn it on, turn it off.
If you unlock it, lock it up.
If you break it, admit it.
If you can't fix it, call in someone who can.
If you borrow it, return it.
If you value it, take care of it.
If you make a mess, clean it up.
If you move it, put it back.
If it belongs to someone else and you want to use it, get
   permission.
If you don't know how to operate it, leave it alone.
If it is none of your business, don't ask questions.
If it isn't broken, don't fix it.
If it will brighten someone's day, say it.
If what you want to say will hurt somebody, zip your lip or say
   it a better way.
If you think you know everything, just open your eyes, look
   around, and realize how little you really know.
If you love someone, show it.
If you need someone, prove it.

What WGACA really boils down to is taking time to calculate the future consequences of your present behavior by anticipating the outcome and result. The classic example of this comes from the world of hockey.

A sportscaster asked Wayne Gretzky, "What makes you the greatest hockey player in the world?"

Gretzky answered, "I'm creative."

The sportscaster was puzzled, "What do you mean, creative?"

Gretzky explained, "Most players go to where the puck is, I go to where the puck is going to be."

What Gretzky is telling us is that the way to succeed and make our dreams come true is to anticipate what would happen in the future and plan our actions accordingly. For, once the possibilities are evaluated and the best way for us to proceed is clear, we must skate as hard and as fast as we can right now, at this instant, and persist in our efforts to score our goals in life.

Someone who knew a lot about goals said the following: "Nothing in this world can take the place of persistence, talent will not—nothing is more common than unsuccessful men and women with talent. Genius will not—unsuccessful geniuses are almost a proverb. Education will not—the world is full of educated derelicts. Persistence and determination alone are omnipotent. The slogan 'press on' has solved and always will solve the problems of the human race."

Wayne Gretzky is a living example of this principle. First he persisted at a young age to find himself, discover what he could do best. Then he anticipated what would happen in his life if he persisted and paid the price today so he could enjoy the price forever. Now, game in and game out, he persists in anticipating where the puck is going to be and persists in scoring his clearly defined goals. His hard work and persistence pays off. He scores more points in a single season than most players do in a career. He holds more individual records than any other hockey player in history and he is only a young man, just getting started. His philosophy must work!

This sounds so easy that perhaps it turns a lot of us off. Sometimes it is hard for us to relate to successful superstars when our world seems so different than theirs. We feel as if we are out of place in this complex society—a custom fit in an off-the-rack world. So what do we do?

The answer is we must take the time to bring life into the kind of terms that we understand. Wayne Gretzky's philosophy does work and it will work for anyone. All we have to do is tailor it to our situation. Then we should be inspired not only to become good but become good for something. Keep in mind the far-reaching implications such as "No matter what your past has been, you have spotless future."; "Never give up on yourself or anyone else—a broken clock is right twice a day."; "If the goal does not assist you to like and love yourself, it is not a good goal.", "Look at yourself and others not for who you are, but for what you have the power to become."; and lastly, "A dime and a twenty dollar gold piece are the same value if they are corroding at the bottom of the ocean. The difference in value comes as we pluck them from the water and use them as they were meant to be used."

Isn't this what life is all about? Discovering ourselves and taking the hand we've been dealt and playing it. We need to take what we have going for us and parlay it into becoming the best we can be. Then, you ask, why these challenges? To bring us back to basics! Football teams that consistently win always go back to basics and work on the fundamentals of blocking and tackling. Salespersons who are successful always concentrate on the basics of product knowledge, prospecting, and simple tried and tested dialogue. Everyday life should be no different!

Therefore, I challenge you to change. Things that don't change remain the same. And things that remain the same become obsolete. I challenge you to accept the challenge to grow and self-improve. Believe in yourself—that you can increase in results, enhance opportunities, and better your family and social lives. And then, I challenge you to follow through by using this challenge and this entire book of challenges as the tool to stimulate and complete the change. A positive change that comes as you understand the procedure:

1. To increase results and achieve success, there must be a behavior modification.

2. Behavior change comes only as we alter and improve our attitude.

3. Attitude change comes from mental conditioning—what goes in the mind must come out.

4. Mental conditioning comes through spaced repetition. When we hear something over and over again, we remember it and implement it into our daily lives. Only then can it become a part of who we are. It has been calculated that we retain only 55 to 65 percent of an idea after six repetitions. So, I again challenge you to read this challenge again. Read and reread this entire book many times—as many times as necessary to retain the information found within its pages. In this way, I guarantee you it will change your life for the best.

Yes, we can make more of a difference and become better today than we were yesterday. Especially if we band together and remember WGACA and set our sights high.

> On top of Old Smokey
> All covered with snow
> I lost my best bird dog
> By aiming too low!

May you develop a passion for what you say and a commitment to whom you say it. May you realize that most integrity is not possible—integrity is not a part-time thing. Integrity is a way of life. You are the message. May you serve society, else your life will be of little value except to yourself. May you understand that this is it. Today is not a dress rehearsal to life. An acorn is not a mentally delinquent oak tree. It is whole and complete, and so are you. Who you are, not what you are, is what makes the difference. May you continually make good memories and throw out your boomerang of unselfish love, kindness, and caring that it all may come back to you.

I, Grandfather, challenge you to accept this philosophy and live by it. May the "force" be with you always as you weather the storm, and may you stay forever young!

* * *

I was excited about trying out this new philosophy from challenge 1, so I took the boomerang and the book and climbed out of the attic to reenter the real world. I decided to keep what I knew to myself. My family finally left Grandmother's house and returned home.

As I took to heart challenge 1, I began to live by WGACA. A noticeable, measurable change occurred in my life. No matter what happened to me, it was hard to be sad. For each time I smiled at someone, he or she always smiled back. Each time I complimented someone, someone complimented me. Each time I built someone up, he or she was eager to help me and build me up. And each time I was tempted to break a rule in school or in athletics, I immediately thought about the consequence of my behavior, that what goes around really does come around, and I was easily swayed away from negative behavior. Amazing! The more I lived WGACA the more I realized how important it was for me to practice what I preached. It eliminated hypocrisy from my life and helped me understand that if the things I believe in and think deeply about are different from the things I do, I will never be happy. It opened my eyes to the fact that if it's a matter of taste—swim with the current, but if it's a matter of principle—stand like a rock. Our values must match our behavior.

And, more important than anything else, living by WGACA caused my mind to contemplate the statement "You were born to succeed." I reflected on this statement a long time wondering what success really is and where is truth found. It was now time to turn to challenge 2.

Challenge 2 was intriguing for it consisted only of instructions on how to find a hidden map. The next day was Saturday, and it finally stopped raining, I rode my bicycle back out to Grandmother's house to start the search.

Following the instructions, I stepped off thirty paces toward the big oak tree in the field, faced the mountain, and jumped up onto a big rock. On the rock was an inscription—the book said it meant "Do not dig, if you won't follow through." I was nervous, but I had come this far so I decided to go on. I found a shovel in Grandmother's shed and began to dig.

Moments later the shovel struck a metal box. My heart started to beat rapidly, and hurriedly I pried open the lid to examine its contents. There it was, the old parchment map pictured in the book. I studied it for a while and then started to read its instructions. I was to go to Los Angeles and find a house in a specific neighborhood in the inner city and talk to an old, wise man. His name was Mapu. In exchange for the boomerang, Mapu would give me challenge 2, *the secret to success and happiness—the explanation of "You Were Born to Succeed."*

I went back into Grandmother's house to look at an atlas to see if I could locate the neighborhood where the old man, Mapu, lived. I finally found the coordinates. It was in the inner city of L.A., just as the map said it was. I called the local shuttle bus service to see how much the fare was. I made a reservation, that, as it turned out, would change my destiny.

I didn't have enough money to take the shuttle to Los Angeles, so I asked my grandmother for it. I negotiated a deal to weed her garden and mow her lawn once a week for the entire summer if she would give me fifty dollars in advance. (I needed money for the hotel, too!) Taking the boomerang, I left Grandmother's house and was on my way to L.A.

When we arrived in the city late Saturday afternoon, the bus driver seemed a bit squirrely. He finally stopped and wouldn't go on. He actually refused to go into the neighborhood I needed to visit and let me out on the corner. The neighborhood seemed calm and I asked a man for directions to Corona Road. The man looked at me like I was crazy, but after constant pleading he finally told me how to get there.

The closer I got to the street, the more I realized I was in a dangerous neighborhood. A car with six guys who didn't look anything like me slowly drove by. They all stared at me and my heart jumped up into my throat. Suddenly the brake lights came on, the doors swung open, and all six guys started screaming and running towards me. Obviously I took off running away from them. I must have broken the world's record in the 100-meter dash because I was burning some heavy-duty rubber as I turned the corner. I headed down an alley, leaped over some garbage cans and scampered up a five-foot chain link fence. I must have run nonstop for twenty minutes until I got away. Now what? In fact, where was I? I was totally lost and it was getting pretty dark.

My fears increased when I heard automatic gunfire from across the way. Women and children started screaming so I immediately turned and ran away from them, trying to find some peace of mind. My mind was racing: What have I done? What have I gotten myself into? Which direction do I run?

As I turned the next corner, I came face to face with another car. I dove behind some giant boxes so that I couldn't be seen. There was a tall fence between me and the road so I felt fairly safe and sat there for a few minutes hoping the headlights wouldn't hit me. My heart was racing faster and faster. The car stopped. Five guys and two girls got out. I noticed that a major drug deal was being made as they passed back and forth some funny-looking white bags and large sums of money. The guys suddenly started laughing, but the girls started crying. I was to witness one of the worst things I've ever seen. The men raped the screaming girls right in front of me. The car sped away. The high fence and barbed wire on top of it made it impossible to climb over to assist the girls. I called to comfort them and said I would find some help.

I got up and ran desperately searching for a pay phone to call the police. About a mile later I found a phone booth but it had been vandalized. A small convenience store was across the street, so I ran for it. I know you won't believe this, but as I arrived at the store, a robbery was just under way. I'm not exaggerating! This neighborhood was the scariest place I've ever been! I dove behind a parked car to hide from the exiting gunmen.

The holdup men ran out and I went inside to again try to call the police. The store clerk had been shot in the arm and leg. I tried to comfort him, helped stop the bleeding and tried to make the call. The phone was ripped out of the wall. Frantically I thumbed through the yellow pages to find some sort of help. I calmed a bit when I saw an ad for a local motel and wrote down the address. The store clerk said it was just down the road, so I raced out the door toward what I thought was safety, a telephone, some warmth and security. At least until morning.

Like a miracle, I found the motel about a mile and a half down the road. I raced into the lobby, told the motel clerk about the incidences and about where they occurred, asked him to call the police, and then registered to get a room so that I could get some sleep. As I registered, the desk clerk looked astonished and bitterly angry. He saw the boomerang in my hand and he became very defensive! I got the feeling that I shouldn't even be there, but where else could I go? I wearily went to my room, lay down on my bed, and did my best to go to sleep.

I couldn't doze off because of the weird feeling I got each time I thought about the evil-looking grin the motel clerk had on his face when I checked in. My fears were confirmed when I heard a groan come from under my bed. At first I was afraid to look. I waited for another noise but it never came. Finally I leaned over to see what was going on. There was a man under my bed—a dead man with a knife stuck in his chest. I had heard his dying breath.

Suddenly there were soft voices outside in the alley. I quickly pulled the dead man up onto the bed, covered him with the blanket, and crawled under the bed. My heart was racing, beating loudly in my head. I could hardly breath as the window slid open. All I could see was a pair of big, black combat boots and a pair of high-top sneakers. The bed shook as I heard four pounds to the dead man's chest, a huge knife fell to the floor, and the two intruders left. I didn't know what to do so I stayed motionless under the bed for the rest of the long, cold, sleepless night.

At the crack of dawn, I scrambled from under the bed, grabbed the boomerang, climbed out the window and I was gone. The street was empty except for a few winos passed out in the park. I must have jogged and walked for thirty minutes when my heart started to beat quickly again. Luckily, this time it was from exhilaration, for the street sign read Corona Road. Hot dog! I had found the old man's street—Mapu's house must be close by.

I began to run from house to house, address to address, madly looking for Mapu's place. Suddenly I felt at ease. For there in front of me was an older home with a faded sign on the front lawn, Mapu's Place.

I scurried up the steps and knocked on the door. No one answered. I again knocked, this time louder! Still no answer. Did I come all this way for nothing? Could it be that the map was obsolete? Perhaps Mapu was dead—(this was a pretty tough neighborhood). I walked around to the back and knocked again. This time a little oriental man answered and opened the door. I asked for Mapu and I was escorted down the hall into a large room.

I needed no introduction for as soon as the six men and six women sitting around the table saw the boomerang in my hand, they immediately stopped talking and stood up in awe. They were amazed and started to cheer. One by one they hugged me, some crying cheers of joy. Mapu, a short, heavy, kind-looking Polynesian man with warm eyes and a gracious smile, was the last to greet me. He stretched out his big arms and said, "Welcome, my son. You're the answer to our suffering. You have brought to us the sacred boomerang from the ancient homeland. Your grandfather's name is Samuel and he is our friend."

Wondering how he knew all this, I replied, "Yes, sir." Mapu said, "Your grandfather is a legend, tutored by the medicine men in Kahada Springs. You are his direct descendant and you have brought us his presence here. Please join our conference. You are our deliverer. You have brought us the 'force.'"

For some reason, I suddenly felt as if what I had just gone through the night before was all worth it. If my boomerang and I were truly needed this much, the ordeal I had endured was really no big deal at all.

There were thirteen chairs around a large table with only twelve people present. An eerie feeling came over me when Mapu said, "Have a seat. We've been channeling in on you and expecting you for a long time."

I sat down and inquired about the boomerang. Mapu explained, "He who owns this sacred boomerang is protected from evil and is filled with the 'force,' deep wisdom, great knowledge, and a special understanding."

Hmmm! This coincided with my grandfather's reputation. Mapu continued, "Have you stopped to think and wonder how you found this place? And why you were protected along your way? It must have been a difficult journey to get here, full of frightening experiences. You are here safely because you own the boomerang."

I asked, "If I have the boomerang, then why haven't I acquired this wisdom and great understanding? When do I get the 'force'?"

Mapu laughed, pointed to the boomerang, and replied, "Remember the inscription? WGACA? What goes around, comes around. The law of the gods requires that once you own the boomerang, you must give it away to receive the 'force.' Your grandfather, Samuel Clark, was ordained many years ago to be a high Kahuna—a keeper of the boomerangs. Only three boomerangs were originally made and your grandfather has given two of them away. This is the last one. The others remained in the homeland and were buried with King Lani O Puoo. I am in line to receive the last boomerang from you."

I was excited because that was why I was there: to give the boomerang to Mapu in exchange for the secret to success and happiness. According to Mapu, I was now in line to receive the full blessings of the boomerang. Wow! What goes around really does come around!

The six men and six women continued with their conference. Lots of races and nationalities were represented, yet the participants all shared love, friendship, and mutual respect. They had no civil rights problems, no hatred between them. Black, Hispanic, Philipino, Japanese, Vietnamese, Korean, Chinese, Tongan, Samoan, Hawaiian, and Caucasian. I watched them interact, and it taught me something most important about human rights.

We can pass all the civil rights legislation in the world, and it still won't change much unless we change the hearts and minds of all the people. Human rights papers with promising words on them mean nothing unless we back up the words with action. These six men and six women— twelve equal human beings—had successfully broken down the barriers of sex, race, color, and creed. They were looking at one another only as human beings, with the right to be free and peaceful and live in pursuit of happiness, love, and success. To see them working together with absolutely no put-downs or discrimination because of what they looked like, was an experience I will never forget.

I believe now with all of my heart that if we keep on keeping on in the human civil rights movement and work toward equality for all, my generation will be the generation that will let freedom ring everywhere! If these folks can do it, so can anyone and everyone! The men were treating the women like ladies (pulling their chairs out and being exceptionally polite and courteous) and at the same time they were treating the women's opinions, viewpoints, and statements exactly as they did their own. The women were treating the men as men. Saying "yes, sir," "no, sir," but treating their opinions the same as they did their own. The women had just as much authority, power, opinion, leadership, and influence as the men! Impressive! They were all on the same level. No distinction between male and female, only bright, intelligent, caring human beings. I realized that this is how it is supposed to be! A woman is equal to a man only when she acts like a woman—and vice versa!! I stopped pondering and turned back into the meeting before I missed something of importance.

These distinguished individuals were the leaders of the twelve outlying communities. The purpose of the meeting was to discuss how they could stop the fierce gang violence, murders, street rapes, stealing, pornography, and the out-of-control drug dealing and abuse that were destroying their communities. Today was the tenth time they had met. Every other session had ended with no answers or solutions to their enormous community problems.

The meeting finally paused for me to make my presentation. I formally presented the boomerang to Mapu following his coaching as he walked and talked me through the step-by-step ancient formal ceremony. When I let go of the boomerang, I thought for sure a bright light would glow out of my finger or a laser beam would cut my hair, but nothing happened. No special feeling, no music, no parade. Nothing. (I guess I watch too much TV!)

However, when Mapu got back to the agenda of the meeting and asked my advice on solving the problem, my mind was opened and a special understanding fell from my lips. I felt a warm feeling come over me and the twelve community leaders were astounded at my wisdom and insight. So was I!! It was obvious that the "force" was with me!

And what was this magnificent oration that was so profound? Nothing new. The "force" simply unveiled to me and reminded all of us that people are inherently good— *born to succeed.* (Oh my gosh, now I was saying it, too!!)

All we need to do is learn to channel the energy into good, clean, pure, powerful, positive, productive, and adventurous actions. Perhaps it was too late to change the tyrants running wild in these communities. We all know it is impossible to change someone until he or she wants to change, but at least we should give him or her the chance. And even if this generation decides not to change, at least the next group of children born into this tough neighborhood will have a fair chance to better their circumstances if we take time to teach them the truisms of success. All they need to know is where to find the secret of success and happiness. (This statement reminded me of the real reason I came to Mapu in the first place.)

I took hold of myself, realized what time it was and said, "I must be going. My grandmother will be worried. But I cannot leave until you answer my questions. Mapu, what is the secret of success and happiness? And where is it found? I came to you to receive challenge 2."

On that note, Mapu stood up and began to speak. "My dear brothers and sisters and young Daniel, the inspiration of the great high Kahuna has allowed the 'force' to be with all of us today. Thank you, Daniel! He has given much to us and we shall give to him; what goes around, comes around. I feel the answer to Daniel's question is the solution to our problem. Yes, you all recall the purpose of our meetings? I believe that the following revelation will suffice to solve our dilemma here and will send young Daniel on his way.

Mapu paused and said to me, "May I now give unto you challenge 2. I have been holding this roll of papyrus for many years. The seal can be broken only with the small end of the boomerang. I now break it in your presence." Mapu held up the ancient scroll and severed the pine gum-coated rope seal. He unrolled the paper and began to speak. "I quote your grandfather."

CHALLENGE 2

You Were Born to Succeed

The Secret to Success And Happiness

So let it be said, so let it be done. From now and forever, by the power of the boomerang that has been bestowed on me by the high Kahuna, the secret to happiness and success—the secret to solving all of our problems will always be found inside—within the heart, mind, and soul of every individual who is willing to look there. For everyone truly is born to succeed.

I, Grandfather, have been in the delivery room of the hospital a few times and have watched the birth of a baby. And you know what? Never once have I seen the baby stand up, head butt the doctor, forearm shiver the nurse, and say, "Come on, doc, you and me, let's play basketball, one on one. I'll take you to the hoop!"

Mothers bring only little boys and girls into the world. Never once have I seen a mother give birth to a doctor, lawyer, educator, mechanic, or a bum. Who we are and what we become is a direct result of the way we have been raised: the influences of our parents, environment, and friendships. Input equals Output 100 percent of the time. We are not born, we are made!

We are born with potential to succeed, and by working hard to develop, polish, and perfect our desires and dreams, we eventually do succeed. We are born with the choice of winning or losing. But it is a choice, and that choice is totally up to us. We are in charge of our destiny and the amount of talent and skill we develop.

Let me ask you a question: When will the world records stop being broken? Never! All Olympic athletes, male and female, believe with all of their hearts that they can run faster, throw farther, and jump higher than ever before. I don't know one of them who would get down into the starting blocks and say, "Oh boy, here goes. I sure hope I take ninth." No, no, no! And because they don't think this negative way and do think positively about their potential to succeed, they will work hundreds of hours perfecting their starts, hundreds of hours perfecting their running form, and hundreds of hours watching videotapes, learning from great coaches and great athletes analyzing their flaws, to become the very best they can possibly be.

Another question to all of us: Why can't we also think like a champion athlete thinks? The answer is, We can! We should! To reach our goal potential and capacity as a human being, we must!! And, sure, most of us will never break a world's record and reach perfection, but in the process of striving for perfection we always obtain excellence and become much more than we thought we could be.

So what is the bottom line? What is challenge 2 about? Challenge 2 is about understanding our human roots, our personal expectations, and our need for positive self-discipline and understanding the importance of following rules. For this is the only way we will ever accept the fact that we were born to succeed and remember that success and happiness are found within. Let me illustrate this point.

Harry Emerson Fosdick said, "No horse gets anywhere until he's harnessed. No steam or gas ever drives anything until it is confined. No Niagara is ever turned unto light and power until it is funneled. No life ever grows great until it is focused, dedicated, and disciplined."

Rules Work for Us

Have you ever felt inadequate, intimidated, or inferior? Have you ever blown it so badly that people are convinced that you are a complete pinecone? Have you ever done something stupid and felt as if your father was so embarrassed by you that he kept the picture that came with the wallet? If so, you are about average. So why do so many of us get so depressed when this occurs? It's because we are too intense. We try too hard. We tighten our muscles and stifle creativity. This causes stress and pressure and we just fall deeper into our depressive rut. For this reason, let's untangle our survival techniques.

Each of us truly was born to succeed. No matter where we came from. We were born with a positive outlook on life. But as we grow older something happens: we change! We become products of our environment—TV, music, friendships, parents, and education. We usually become more and more negative and skeptical. For instance, have you ever heard a child say, "It's impossible"? I never have. But how many adults do we hear say, "It's impossible"? Yes, it's true. Something happens between birth and adulthood. Something colors our positive outlook. We let negativism creep into our minds. Ask yourself, why am I the way that I am? What has happened to me? Are you more positive than the person sitting next to you at work or school? Or are you more negative than that person? There must be a reason why. As you are evaluating yourself to see if you are more positive or negative than you were a few years ago, let me take us back to our childhood. Back to when we knew we could do it all. When we had no doubt that we could have whatever we dreamed about. Back to when we knew we were born to succeed. When obstacles played no part in our perfection process.

Christopher's Adventure

I was at my friend's home one day and witnessed what all of us used to be like. I was sitting on the sofa, watching my friend's young nine-month-old baby boy, who was just beginning to crawl. His name was Christopher and he had noticed a big red doll sitting on a chair on the other side of the room. I could tell he had made up his mind to go over and get it. You could see in his eyes he knew he could get the doll. He slithered off the chair where he was sitting, crashed to the floor, and with his eyes fixed on the doll, started to crawl. He ran smack into a table. But that was no problem for Christopher. He didn't even blink an eye. He just moved to the side and kept crawling.

Christopher got to the sofa where I was sitting and hiked up the side. Across the sofa he scooted with an awesome breaststroke. In a hurry, he flipped off the end of the sofa and landed on his head. Although it looked as if he had broken his neck, he didn't blink an eye. He knew he could get the big red doll—he kept crawling. He ran into another chair. No problem, he just ducked under it. Finally he got to his destination: the chair where the doll was sitting. He grabbed the leg of the chair and started to rock it. The doll began to teeter back and forth, back and forth. Christopher struggled, he reached, he stretched. He was two inches from the doll's foot when a heartbreaking scene took place. The babysitter came into the room from the kitchen. Seeing what was going on, she started to walk across the room toward him. "Christopher, no!" She picked him up and took him all the way back across the room and put him back in the chair from where he had started this long journey. She thought that would solve everything. Question: Did it solve everything? *No way!*

The second the babysitter turned her back, Christopher's head whipped around and once again he focused his gaze on the big red doll. And with that look that said: "Yes, I can accomplish my goal. No matter how many obstacles are thrown in my way, I can make my dreams come true," Christopher again slid off the chair, onto the floor and began his journey with even greater desire and fortitude. You could see it in his eyes. He knew he could get the doll!

What has happened to us? When we were Christopher's age we thought and believed exactly the way he did. There was a time in every one of our lives when we knew we could do it all. Why have we changed? Why has it become so difficult for us to face our obstacles head-on, deal with them, and move toward making our dreams come true? The answer lies in uncovering three keys to success. First, we have run out of motivation.

I used to own a Volkswagon beetle. It was a pretty good car only because I spent several hundred dollars fixing it up. One day I got into my car to drive to the city. It started right up. I backed out of the garage and then it stalled. I tried to turn it over for five minutes. It wouldn't start. Needless to say I was ticked off at this stupid car. (Notice that the car was stupid—not I!) I got out, slammed the door, stormed into the house, picked up some other keys, got into another car, and backed it around the Volkswagon and went on my way. I was so ticked off! I refused to spend any more money on this stupid car. So I let it sit there. Thirty-one days went by. Weeds began to grow underneath it. Finally, the inconvenience of backing around the car got to me, so I broke down and paid a mechanic to come to my house to fix it. He opened the tiny hood in the back, stuck his fingers in, twisted something, closed the hood, looked up at me after a half minute of work and said, "Mr. Clark, you have run out of gas." I was shocked and obviously embarrassed. For thirty-one days that car had been sitting there mechanically sound and all it lacked was gas!

Human beings are exactly the same way. Most of us are mechanically sound. Most of us work perfectly in every way. All we lack is motivation. Most of those whose lives aren't going anywhere have simply run out of motivation.

The second key to success is our need for basic direction. We need a formula that transfers our motivation into desirable action. Usually this formula is referred to as a rule book or a set of rules.

Rules—The Key to Success

A football field has an out-of-bounds line on one side of the field and one on the other side. We play the game by the rules in-between the sidelines. Because we play the game to win and you can't win if you are out-of-bounds (you must be on the game field and play by the rules). It doesn't make sense if the player runs out-of-bounds on purpose. Life is the same way. If we know what the rules and out-of-bounds lines are in life (work, school, classroom, family life) and break them on purpose and continually run out-of-bounds, how in the world can we possibly expect to win our share of the time? It just doesn't make sense!

A high-school all-American was kicked off his team for drinking. He was depressed and ticked off at the coach. His parents went to the superintendent to pull some strings and get their son reinstated on the team. Everyone was blaming the coach.

I asked the suspended player if he knew it was against the rules to drink during the season. He said, "Yes." I asked, "Then who kicked whom off the team?" The coach didn't kick him off the team, he kicked himself off the team! He had a choice: he knew the rules and he chose to break them.

Each of us was born to succeed. The only way we can give ourselves a fair chance to win and succeed is if we stay in-bounds and always choose to obey the rules. The quarterback of the San Francisco 49ers doesn't hand the ball off to his favorite running-back to have him run out-of-bounds. That is not the object of the game. He is supposed to stay inbounds and strive to score a touchdown so the 49ers can win. If he doesn't do so, no one on his team, in the league, or in the world for that matter, will respect him. Do people respect you? If you don't play you can't win! People respect winners! People like to do business with winners!!

Some of us hate the very word *rules*. Even these simple suggestions cause us to inwardly rebel, and admit, "I won't follow them and let them curtail my freedom. I don't want my parents giving me curfews that will turn me into mom's little lambie pie. I want to be *me*. I don't want anybody else to ever tell me what to do. Rules aren't for me. Rules are to be broken."

Do you relate to this? If you do, we must start to think a new way. Analyze kite flying. It will start us in this rethinking process and help us better understand the second key to success, which is a need for basic direction provided by rules, and will now introduce the third key to success: obeying the rules.

I watched as a young boy flew a kite under the direction of his father. He asked, "Dad, what holds the kite up?"

"The string." his father replied.

"No, Dad, the string holds the kite down, not up."

His father challenged, "If you think so, let go of the string."

The boy let go of the string, and sure enough the kite began to fall. Doesn't this seem odd? The very thing that appears to keep the kite down is actually what keeps it up. This is also true in life. Those strings that are tied to us, those rules and regulations that seem to hold us down and take away our freedoms, are actually holding us up and allowing us to climb higher toward becoming the best that we can be.

Rules, regulations, and cautious reprimands really do help us succeed, sometimes in ways we don't realize until later.

One evening I was at my grandson's home. We were all

sitting in the family room enjoying some good music in the warmth of a blazing fire. My grandson's nine-month-old daughter was playing on the floor when the fire caught her eye. She was fascinated by the flames, the beautiful colors, and the sparks, and she started to crawl toward the fireplace. Because her father loved her very much and knew something about the fire she did not know, my grandson excused himself, got up from his chair (it sure was an inconvenience, but his love prevailed), and he walked across the room to retrieve little Mary Kathryn. He carried her back to the safety of her toys, put her back on the floor, and again enjoyed our conversation.

Ten minutes went by. Mary Kathryn again began to crawl toward the fascinating flames with a determined, playful gleam in her eye. Once again my grandson got up from his comfortable chair and walked across the room to stop Mary Kathryn from burning herself. Because he knew something that she did not know—because he loved her very, very much—he gently patted her bottom as he carried her back to her toys and sternly said, "No Mary Kathryn, you can't play in the fire. You're going to get burned."

She started to cry and was probably thinking, "Dad, you jerk. You are so conservative and old-fashioned. Why won't you let me play in the fire? Everyone else's parents let them play in the fire! I'll show you when you're not around. I'm a big girl, and I don't need you to tell me what to do."

Pause and ask yourself, regardless of your age, do you sometimes feel this way? Do you rebel against authority and people who tell you what to do simply because you want to establish and maintain your individuality? Think about your situation. There is always someone around you who knows more than you know and who can share that knowledge with you in a positive way. It doesn't seem right or intelligent if we don't take the time to listen to what they have to say and follow their advice. Many people know more than we know. As a result of their concern for us they know that we will get burned if they don't share their knowledge with us.

In business, company leaders and experienced sales trainers know more than we do, so we should follow their advice. At home, our parents know more than we know, so we should follow their counsel and curfews. In school, our teachers and coaches know more than we do. We should, therefore, accept their counsel and advice as they steer us away from the fires of life. They simply want to share their experience, with their trials and errors, so that our lives will be easier and we won't get burned. Rules don't curtail us, they set us free! When followed, rules keep us on course, keep us from wasting time and keep us organized and disciplined so that we can accomplish our goals.

Athletes, for instance, become champions only through discipline and strict adherence to regimented rules. An athlete becomes totally free to use all of his speed and agility only after he or she has followed the training rules and paid the price on the practice field. The athlete must get his or her body in tip-top muscular and cardiovascular condition. There are certainly athletes who can break rules and make it in the short run. There are also businessmen and businesswomen who can break rules and make it in the shortrun. But what goes around comes around. And if it is ultimate success that we truly want, in the long run only the disciplined and rule keepers become successful.

Join with me and let us not rebel against wisdom, experience, and authority. Remember what Emerson said, "Our chief want in life is to find somebody who'll make us do what we can." When we do find someone like this, we live up to our birthright promise because we have others to help us act as if we were born to succeed. What's the bottom line?

"Only as high as I reach can I grow;
Only by keeping the rules can I go;
Only as deep as I look can I see;
Only as much as I dream can I be."

If there is an underlying theme and connecting thread running through challenge 2, it is the fact that every person can succeed if he or she looks inside for happiness and wants to work hard enough. No one should ever settle for anything else, therefore, than the very best from himself or herself, from his or her friends, from his or her family, and from life itself. Take charge of your life. And don't leave important things to chance. Always remember, you were born to succeed! I, Grandfather, challenge you to accept this philosophy and live by it. May the "force" be with you always as you weather the storm, and may you stay forever young!

Mapu's amazing exhortation had ended. He had just given me challenge 2. It was time for me to go. We stood and I hugged each woman and man good-bye. The neighborhood obviously scared away policemen, shuttle drivers, and cab drivers, so the Oriental man who had answered the door drove me back to the L.A. airport so I could catch the shuttle. I arrived back at Grandmother's home Sunday afternoon to a worried grandparent, sick parents, and a house full of friends and police. I knew they wouldn't believe me if I told them what had happened to me and where I had been. Besides, the *Book of Challenges* was sacred and secret, only for me to know about. Therefore, I sluffed off the questions and went to my room. Exhausted, I immediately fell asleep. Tomorrow I would get the sacred wood-covered book back out of the chest so I could study it some more. I was eager to start living challenge 2 and move on to challenge 3.

Early the next morning I quickly climbed into the attic.

I opened up the chest to insert the papyrus scroll of challenge 2 into the space provided, and saw, much to my surprise, the book was already mysteriously opened to challenge 3. It puzzled me. Challenge 3 consisted only of a few lines. It simply said, "The 'Force' is with you—Find the 'F.O.R.C.E.' Swimming pool is near—have no fear—Doug Davis you will find and he will mold your mind with the 'F.O.R.C.E.' peace of mind."

I had never seen *F.O.R.C.E.* spelled as an acronym, so I immediately sought to discover what this word symbolized and what the rhyme meant. I put the book back into the chest and hurried outside to find a local swimming pool.

What a shock. There were five local swimming clubs in Grandmother's area. I visited every one of them and there was absolutely no sign of the "F.O.R.C.E.," Mr. Doug Davis, nor anyone or anything else for that matter. No information, no "F.O.R.C.E.," and no one except an old gardener at each location. But what did they know? I was frustrated! What could these old men possibly tell me?

Deeply disappointed, I started back to Grandmother's house, when suddenly, curiosity steered me back to the swimming clubs. For some reason, I thought I better recheck each location just in case someone had just, by chance, stopped by with the answer to my questions. As I retraced my steps, the first pool was still empty except for the same old gardener standing outside. Totally beside myself, I yelled out and momentarily broke down my prejudice, "Do you know anything about the 'F.O.R.C.E.'?"

The gardener was a large Polynesian man with a big smile. He waved me inside and I followed him into the pool. He looked deep into my eyes and in broken English asked, "How bad you want know about 'F.O.R.C.E.'?"

I replied, "Real bad."

He yelled at me, "Obviously not bad enough," and pushed me into the pool. He dove in on top of me and held my head under the water until I started to violently kick and swing and desperately strike out for freedom. It must have been at least a minute before he finally let me up and helped me out of the water. I was frightened and gasping for air. I yelled at him, "What did you do that for?"

He smiled and laughed and answered me, "Until you want to know about the 'F.O.R.C.E.' as much as you wanted air, you will not value it nor use it in your everyday life. Now, I ask again, "Do you want to know about the 'F.O.R.C.E.'?" I took a deep breath and gasped, "Yes. Yes, I do! And I'll fight you for it!!"

He politely answered, "F stands for *focusing*. A swimming pool is near, have no fear. Doug Davis you will find, and he will mold your mind."

Wow, he knew the rhyme. He helped me dry off and gave me a change of clothes. I promptly backtracked to the second swimming club I had previously visited. Out in front was a different gardener. I stopped and asked him, "Excuse me, do you know anything about the 'F.O.R.C.E.'?"

He was a muscular man from Fiji who also had a big smile. He politely answered, "O stands for *on*. A swimming pool is near, have no fear, Doug Davis you will find . . ." (Holy Cow. He also knew the rhyme!) I obviously ran to the third pool I had previously visited to find another gardener. I figured I was on a roll and would soon find the answer to my dilemma. I hurried, hoping he was still there, and sure enough, as I approached the gardener, he smiled as if he was expecting me.

He was a native Hawaiian man with, you guessed it, a big smile. When I asked him about the F.O.R.C.E. he quietly spoke up, "R is for *reality*." He then quoted the rhyme. I rushed to find the fourth gardener. On the way over I realized something very profound.

How many times in life do we miss an opportunity in life to succeed? How many times in life do we miss an opportunity to learn and grow and develop and mature and improve simply because we think we know it all. We therefore, refuse to talk and interact with those not in our own social class. John Wooden said, "It's what we learn after we know it all that brings us success." Wow, think about this. He's right and I had been blowing it badly. I had refused to talk and listen to these gardeners for no other reason except for the fact that they were gardeners. I had prejudged them, thinking I was more knowledgeable and better than they were simply because they didn't have my parents' money, nice clothes, a college education, and fine cars. Suddenly I was embarrassed and filled with shame. It hit me square in the face and straight to the heart: Every person truly is important and worthwhile. Every person knows something that I do not know. Every person will be missed when he or she is gone. Every person has a right to do what he or she wants to do and be who he or she wants to be. A person's personal happiness is what it's all about. Sure, I need to encourage people to be good, clean, pure, powerful and positive; but I need to live and let live.

I finally reached the fourth swimming club but it was too late, the gardener was gone. I suddenly realized something else fundamental about life and relationships. I needed this gardener! He had something I needed and apparently I had let the opportunity slip by. He had something of incredible value that only he could provide, and I needed this man desperately for who he was and what he had inside of him, not for what he did for a job or what he looked like on the outside. I hope I've learned this lesson for life!

I heard a loud noise and frantically ran to the back of the building to see what it was. To my pleasant surprise, there he was sitting in a wheelchair reading a book. It turned out the book was written in Russian! This time I didn't just ask about the force, I wanted to know about him. For the first time in my life, I realized the importance of every individual and I didn't want to miss another one of life's seminars.

He was a proud Tongan man, and, like all the other

gardeners, he, too, had a big smile. He was very old and he didn't have any legs. I was so overcome, I had to find out what happened to him. He answered he had lost both legs in World War II. He seemed exceptionally intelligent, so I asked him why he was just a gardener. He raised his voice and eloquently exclaimed, "I am not 'just' a gardener. This is what I choose to do with my life and with my time and talents." He continued, "I almost feel 'called' to do it. Dr. Martin Luther King, Jr., said, 'It doesn't matter what a man does if he does it well. If a man is called to be a street sweeper, he should sweep streets even as Michelangelo painted or Beethoven composed music or Shakespeare wrote poetry. He should sweep streets so well that all the hosts of heaven and earth will pause to say "Here lived a great street sweeper, a leader in his field, who did his job well." "

He continued to scold me, "Please don't judge me for what I do, but for how I do it. I do an honest day's work for an honest day's pay. And I enjoy being a gardener. I have an MBA degree from Harvard University, and my doctorate is in philosophy from the University of California at Berkeley. I am qualified and educated and could do pretty much what I willed, where I wanted to do it, with whichever company I chose. I was a successful college professor and then a highly paid corporate man for many years, but now I choose to be a gardener. And please notice, look around, I am a pretty darn good gardener if I do say so myself!"

I agreed and complimented him on the beautiful, colorful flower beds; manicured bushes; and carefully pruned trees. (Incidentally, I had been in so much of a hurry before that I hadn't noticed this either. There must be a lesson in this somewhere, such as, "Take time to smell the roses and see the beauty in nature. You only pass by this way but once.")

I was just about ready to ask him what he knew about the "force," when I decided to ask one more question about him that had been bugging me. Because he had no legs,

I had a strong urge to know what he thought about war. War has been in the news for so many years and throughout so many generations, and this gentleman seemed so peaceful and wise and so in tune with life, I wanted to know his opinion. When I inquired, he immediately stared away and let tension fill the air. After about five minutes of dead silence (which seemed like an eternity), he finally began to speak.

"Before I joined the army and went to war, I used to swear all the time. I had the filthiest, most vulgar mouth in the whole world. I thought by being in the army and fighting the Nazis and everything, I would probably come home swearing better than ever before. But since I've been home, I haven't sworn once. I haven't even had the urge to. I have definitely mellowed out as a result of war. I guess it was because I was around Don Samson too long. Don never swore, and when you were around him, you never wanted to swear either because it made you feel funny, like you were swearing around a little girl or a minister or something.

"I suppose you probably think this guy really was a sissy. At the beginning of boot camp, a lot of the fellows used to tease him about being too nice of a guy. The teasing never got under his skin, so all of the guys soon left him alone. All except big Chuck Williams, the platoon bully. Don was small but strong and exceptionally athletic. Chuck was large and cocky—the kind of guy who would put bricks in guys' packs when we went on forty-mile hikes. Everyone was chicken to fight big Chuck, so he remained undisturbed in playing his stupid tricks until one day he went a little too far. While Don was out getting a haircut, Chuck drew a mustache on the picture he had of his best friend. I knew Don wouldn't like this, but everyone was afraid to tell him to stop. Then Don walked in. 'Who did this?' Don calmly asked. Cocky, big Chuck Williams answered, 'I did. What are you going to do about it?' "

"I don't think it was more than a second from the time

Chuck finished his sentence until Don proceeded to give him the beating of his life. No one interfered. The lieutenant rushed in to stop the fight, but when he saw who was getting the worst of it, he left—not interfering.

"Don never became great friends with anyone. He always kept people at a distance. But everyone respected him. We used to kid around that we would probably pray to him if we didn't know better. Everyone was in awe of Don Samson's principles, values, inner strength, and total peace of mind.

"Even though Don was mellow, he definitely was not a passive soldier. When it came to fighting the enemy, he was the first one to volunteer for the frightening, terrifying missions. In fact, every single one of the men on my platoon had Don save his life at least once. Don was a true hero, not just to those who knew him, but for America! He was a very well-decorated soldier at the end of the war."

The old gardener continued, "This is all wonderful, but this is not why I chose to tell you about Don Samson. He not only positively affected the lives of those of us in the platoon, but he helped each of us put war into proper perspective.

"Because Don was a true war hero in every sense of the word, you would think that he would receive many promotions and become a high-ranking officer during the war. To the contrary. The officers were afraid to promote Don because he had the reputation for being a German-lover. He didn't hate the Germans like everyone else. He said they were about the same as us, perhaps a little bit more hard-headed, but they were basically the same. He said they had wives and girlfriends and families who loved them and prayed for their well-being just like we do! Don was not only empathetic toward the people, but he spoke excellent German, too. Just before the war broke out, Don had attended college for three years in Germany and had had a German roommate.

"I often wondered if Don liked the Germans so much, why was he able to fight them so well? I finally asked him, and he simply replied, 'The only way to stop Hitler and his Nazis is to defeat the German people who have let themselves be deceived by Hitler.' He said it was wrong to kill the Germans but it was more wrong for Hitler and his Nazis to destroy and deceive the rest of the world. Don said we are sometimes forced to choose between two evils, and Hitler had to be stopped at all cost!

"Once, Don stayed up all night trying to help save the life of a young German soldier boy who had a bullet in his chest. The boy died early the next morning, and I know I saw a tear in Don's eyes as he began digging the grave.

"The final story of Don and the true story of war happened another night a few months later. That night the platoon next to us caught a German trying to steal supplies. In catching him, one of our men was injured. The German was brought to our camp on the way to the brig. He'd been brought before the captain and sentenced to be shot at dawn. As the night wore on, we were all sitting around a fire talking about home and wondering if we would ever see it again. Suddenly, as the light of the fire reflected on the prisoner's face, Don sprang to his feet. The visible muscles of his neck and arms were bulging and tense. He shook his head and blinked his eyes to confirm what he thought he saw. Then he sprang toward the German. My first reaction was to protect the German. It wasn't uncommon for soldiers to try and kill a prisoner, remembering one of their buddies who had been killed by the Germans. But in this instance, that was not the case. Before anyone had a chance to do anything, Don and the prisoner were clasping each others arms hugging and kissing each other on the cheek as they said a few things in German. Everyone was stunned and watched in amazement. Everyone except the guard, who shouted, 'Weiterlaufen, schwein.' The German broke Don's grip and began walking again to the brig.

The guard looked at Don and said, 'You ought to be shot, you pig-lover.'

"All that kept Don from smashing the guard in the mouth was his deeply instilled respect for authority. He turned around. You could see every muscle quivering and his fists clenched so tightly that the blood was forced out of them. He sat back down and just stared at the ground.

"I guess the captain got word of this little episode because a few minutes later Don was ordered to report immediately to his tent. Tents are not very soundproof and everyone within the immediate vicinity clearly heard as the captain ordered Don to be the fifth man on the sunrise firing squad.

"When Don came out of the tent, I asked what he was going to do. I reminded him that refusing to obey a direct order meant that he would be shot himself. Don said, 'I understand the consequence, but how can I shoot my best friend, the only man I had as a roommate in college? How can I shoot a man my family loves? A man who is close to his family, a man who has actually changed my life for the best.' "

The old Tongan gardener paused and then began to stare. Five minutes went by, perhaps longer. It again seemed like an eternity. I finally interrupted him and asked, "What did Don do?"

The gardener smiled and replied, "Before I tell you the rest of the story, what do you think you would have done?"

I thought for a minute and decided: "It would be hard to shoot your friend, but the German was going to die whether I decided to shoot or not. My refusing to shoot would have just meant that two men would die instead of one. What good would I be to my country if I was dead?"

The Tongan interrupted me, "That is true. But what kind of life would you have had if you knew you had shot your best friend in cold blood?"

I argued back, "You don't understand. If Don chose to take part in the firing squad, he wouldn't have been guilty of the German's death. The German would have been the victim of martial law operating through Don. If taking part on the firing squad would make Don responsible for this man's death, Don should also be responsible for the death of every other German he killed in the war whom he didn't know."

The Tongan again interrupted and said, "Maybe you are right, Daniel. But if I were on a firing squad to shoot you, I wouldn't shoot. No matter who told me to or no matter who would be held responsible. Would you shoot me if you were ordered to? Would you shoot your own brother if you were ordered to?"

I thought for a while and answered, "If I were to be shot by a firing squad and you were on the firing squad, I would want you to shoot. I would want my brother to shoot. It is better that one die instead of two. Would it be easier on Mom and Dad if both of us got killed instead of just one of us?"

"If I were Mom or Dad," said the Tongan gardener, "I think I would rather have both of my boys dead than have one shoot the other in cold blood."

The Tongan man paused and then started to cry. "Don was shot together with the German the next morning."

Five minutes of dead silence passed while we both sat motionless crying and contemplating war versus the relationships of loyal friends.

The gardener continued, "The day after Don was shot, the men in our platoon were so upset that most of us lost our cool and our presence of mind. We were walking through the woods on a mission and didn't notice the booby trap in front of us. Three of us at the front of the line lost our legs in the explosion of the mine. You see, Don influenced us not only while he was alive, he also influenced us after he had died. It is my goal to live a Don-like life. If there was ever a saint, Don Samson was one and I will always love him dearly.

"My vision of war is that war is not necessary. It is evil. Nothing good comes of it. As long as we do not start wars, we will be okay. But if by chance a warring country attacks us and wants to take away what matters most, no one in his or her right mind should ever stand aside and say, 'No problem; what is mine is yours.' There comes a time when every man and every woman must stand up for what he or she believes in and fight to the end. I would rather lose my legs and live with liberty than to live with peace at the expense of my freedom. Obviously, sometimes war is necessary and we must go and fight."

The elderly Tongan gardener continued with that big warm smile and said, "I know you have come to ask about the 'force,' and before I give you my letter as part of the master Kahuna plan, let me just challenge you myself. Take the 'force' and use it to bring about peace and freedom throughout the world."

He paused and then offered the information about the "force!" "My letter is C. C stands for causes." And then he quoted the rhyme. I thanked him and flew out of there on a beeline to the last pool. Holy cow! I must have been at this fourth swimming club for over an hour! I sprinted toward the fifth pool hoping I wasn't too late!

Before I arrived it started to rain, so when I got there I immediately waved to the gardener inside to open the door. He was sitting by his wife and motioned me to come in as if he were waiting for me. I was soaked. He offered me his shawl and he and his wife invited me upstairs to share their warm fire.

We climbed some steep steps, turned down a long, cedar corridor, and walked about 200 yards high in the air to a back room that he called home. Hanging on the wall of his home were two pictures, one of my Grandfather Clark and the other of a man I didn't know. The caption under the unidentified picture read, Doug Davis—Explorer, Engineer, Entrepreneur, Land Developer, Miner, Successful Businessman, Successful Philosopher, Outstanding Father. (Ah, hah; I finally found Mr. Davis!)

Warming to the fire, I asked this very old and wise Maori

man what he knew about the "force." He smiled and answered, "E stands for energy. Let me now fulfill the rhyme." He did and then continued.

"F.O.R.C.E. is the acronym that means Focusing On Reality Causes Energy. Interpreted it means if you take care of business right now and concentrate all your efforts on the *now,* you become possessed with the force that enables you to reach beyond your performance and excel beyond your wildest dreams. The 'force' is nothing more than a concentrated, focused, burning desire to be the very best you can possibly be right now. It is working where you are, with what you have, creating intense energy within you to endure and excel in those things you pursue."

I asked him if he could give me challenge 3, and he said no. He handed me an old notepad and explained, "Challenge 3 was left by your grandfather in the form of the blessing to this man Doug Davis." He pointed to the picture on the wall. "Among other things, your grandfather blessed Doug Davis with a keen sense of wonderment and an exceptional business mind to take a calculated risk. Using this blessing, Doug Davis now lives in Utah and has become a walking and talking system of success. This notepad is challenge 3. It was written and compiled by Doug Davis himself and came about as a result of his many adventures, experiences, and dollar deals. It is entitled, 'Thoughts On the Business of Life.' It's sub-head reads 'LEATHY,' which means, 'Always to remember— Never to Forget'.

"Challenge 3 is a rare and valuable collection of exactly seventy-five quotable quotes on many vital issues that pertain to life, liberty, true success, and lasting happiness. You may now have the pad for your forever-safe keeping, Daniel. This is the original, written in Doug Davis's own handwriting, sealed with the sacred seal of the great high Kahuna by your grandfather. Protect and cherish this pad by keeping it in the sacred book. Cherish the information within its pages. Study it, digest it, and cherish the amazing wisdom found on its worn wrinkled pages. Read and reread it and memorize it so it can be a part of who you are!"

I thanked the gardener and walked back to Grandmother's house. Being careful not to damage the note pad containing challenge 3, I meticulously slid it into the space provided in the sacred book. I then hid the book back in the chest in the attic and went straight to bed.

Bright and early the next morning, I jumped out of bed, sneaked up to the attic and removed the book, and locked myself in my room. It was now time for me to improve myself through challenge 3.

Challenge 3

"LEATHY—Always to Remember, Never to Forget"

Thoughts on the Business of Life by Doug Davis

Leadership

There are no bad boys; only bad training, bad environment, bad thinking, bad example, and poor leadership. Good leadership is the art of getting someone else to do something that you want done because he wants to do it.

Getting It

Too many young people itch for what they want without scratching for it.

Either I will find a way or I will make one.

Feelings

Feelings are not right or wrong—they just are. We shouldn't try to control our feelings. We need to control our actions. It's OK to feel happy or sad, angry, depressed, lonely, discouraged, exhilarated, or like jumping for joy. We just need to channel our feelings into positive actions.

Discipline

Perhaps the most valuable result of life is the ability to make yourself do the thing you have to do when it has to be done, whether you like it or not.

Focusing

Every industrious man in every lawful calling is a useful man. And one principle reason why men are so often useless is that they neglect their own profession or calling and divide and shift their attention upon a multiplicity of objects and pursuits.

Never give a man up until he has failed at something he likes.

Habits

When we have practiced good actions a while, they become easy. When they are easy, we take pleasure in them. When they please us, we do them frequently. And then by frequency of act, they grow into strong cables of habit. The long span of the bridge of your life is supported by countless cables that you are spinning now and that is why today is such an important day. Make the cables good, clean, and strong.

Attitude

Sunshine is delicious. Rain is refreshing. Wind is bracing. Snow is exhilarating. You see, there is no such thing as bad weather; there are only different kinds of good weather.

A great many people think they are thinking when they are simply rearranging their prejudices.

Merely having an open mind is nothing. The object of

opening the mind (like of opening the mouth) is to shut it again on something solid.

The Constitution of America only guarantees the pursuit of happiness. You have to catch up with it yourself. Fortunately, happiness is something that depends not on position but on disposition. Life is what you make it.

Life

It is not so important to be serious as it is to be serious about the important things.

It is with life as with a play: It matters not how long the action is spun out, but how good the acting is.

Someone has well said, "Success is a journey, not a destination." Happiness is to be found along the way, not at the end of the road. For then the journey is over and it is too late. Today, this hour, this minute in the day, each of us needs to sense the fact that life is good with all its trials and troubles and perhaps more interesting because of them.

It is a poor and disgraceful thing not to be able to reply with some degree of certainty to the simple questions: What will you be? What will you do? Where are you going?

Love

"Love is a commitment, not a way of feeling."

Luck

What helps luck is a habit of watching for opportunities, of having a patient but restless mind, of sacrificing one's ease or vanity, of uniting a love of detailed foresight, and of passing through hard times bravely and cheerfully.

Shortcuts

"Do it the long, hard way! Think ahead of your job, then nothing in the world can keep the job ahead from reaching out for you. Do it better than it needs to be done. Next time, doing it will be child's play. Let no one or anything stand between you and the difficult task. Let nothing deny you this rich chance to obtain strength by adversity, confidence by mastery, success by deserving it. Do it better each time. Do it better than anyone else can do it. I know this may sound old-fashioned; it is. But it has built the world."

Happiness

"We have no more right to consume happiness without producing it than to consume wealth without producing it."

True enjoyment comes from activity in the mind and exercise of the body. The two are ever united.

May we never let the things we can't have or don't have or shouldn't have spoil our enjoyment of the things we do have and can have. As we value our happiness, let us not forget it. For one of the greatest lessons in life is learning to be happy without the things we cannot or should not have.

Rich

"If you want to know how rich you really are, find out what would be left of you tomorrow if you should lose every dollar you own tonight."

The happiness of life is made up of minute fractions: the little soon-forgotten charities of a kiss or smile, a kind look, a heartfelt compliment, and the countless infinitesimals of pleasurable and genial feelings.

If you are not rich, notice how you make yourself poor.

The question for each man to settle is not what he would do if he had means, time, influence, and educational advantages; but what he will do with the things he does have.

Experience

Fool me once, shame on you; fool me twice, shame on me.

Nothing is a waste of time if you use the experience wisely.

Humor

A boy becomes a man and grows up the day he has his first good laugh—at himself. He who laughs—lasts!

True Education

A young man who has the combination of the learning of books with the learning that comes from doing things with the hands, need not worry about getting along in the world today or at any time.

One pound of learning requires ten pounds of common sense to apply it.

Almost all men are intelligent; it is method that they lack.

Common Sense

Common sense is the knack of seeing things as they are and doing things as they ought to be done.

Work

In no direction that we turn should we expect ease or comfort. If we are honest and we have the will to win, we find only danger, hard work, and iron resolution.

Some people are willing to work only if they can start at the top and work up?!

We have employments assigned to us for every circumstance in life. When we are alone, we have our thoughts to watch; in the family, our tempers; and in company, our tongues.

The rung of a ladder was never meant to rest upon, but only to hold, a man's foot long enough to enable him to put the other somewhat higher.

We work day after day not to finish things but to make the future better because we will spend the rest of our lives there.

Decision Making

When, against one's will, one is high-pressured into making a hurried decision, the best answer is always no. No is more easily changed to yes than yes is changed to no.

Thinking well is wise, planning well wiser, doing well wisest and best of all.

Opportunity

Four things come not back: the spoken word, the sped arrow, past life, and neglected opportunity.

We all have to learn in one way or another that neither men nor boys get second chances in this world. We all get new chances until the end of our lives, but not second chances in the same set of circumstances. And the great difference between one person and another is how he takes hold and uses his first chance and how he takes his fall if it is scored against him.

Perception

The world is governed more by appearances than by realities, therefore, it is as necessary to seem to know something as to know it.

What we see depends mainly on what we look for.

Self-Esteem

Others can stop you temporarily; only you can do it permanently.

Reality

If you worry about what may be and wonder what might have been, you will ignore what is.

Blame

When you blame others, you give up your power to change and self-improve.

Progress

If you find a good solution and become attached to it, the solution becomes your next problem.

Right and Wrong

There is no right or wrong, only consequences. You are the cause of everything that happens to you. Be careful what you cause.

Fear

Feelings of inferiority and superiority are the same. They both come from fear.

What you are afraid to do is a clear indicator of the next thing you need to do.

Worry

Worry means not making a decision. The sooner we make a decision and act, the sooner worry leaves us. Worry comes from the belief that you are powerless.

Service

The smallest good deed is better than the grandest good intention.

What we have done for ourselves alone dies with us. What we have done for others and the world remains and is immortal.

Beware of too much service. When you have a constant need to help other people, notice how and why you must keep them helpless.

Friends

Make no man your friend before inquiring how he has used his former friends, for you must expect him to treat you as he has treated them. Be slow to give your friendship; but when you have given it, strive to make it lasting, for it is as reprehensible to make many changes in one's associates as to have no friends at all. Either test your friends to your own injury or be willing to forego a test of your companions.

The making of friends who are real friends is the best token we have of a man's success in life.

Anger

The greatest remedy for anger is delay.

Management

No matter how much work a man can do, no matter how engaging his personality may be, he will not advance far in business if he cannot work through others.

The question, Who ought to be boss? is like asking, Who ought to be the tenor in a quartet? Obviously the man who can sing tenor.

It is with narrow-souled people as with narrow-necked bottles: The less they have in them, the more noise they make in pouring it out.

Communication

Remember, every time you open your mouth to talk, your mind walks out and parades up and down the words.

Let us keep our mouths shut and our pens dry until we know the facts.

The world abhors closeness and all but admires extravagance, yet a slack hand shows weakness and a tight handshake, strength.

Most of the time we don't communicate, we just take turns talking.

The more noise a man or motor makes, the less power there is available.

Talk happiness; the world is sad enough without your woe.

Opinions

He who wrestles with us strengthens our nerves and sharpens our skill. Our antagonist is actually our helper.

Every man has a right to his opinion, but no one has a right to be wrong in his facts.

Obstacles

It is a good rule to face difficulties at the time they arrive and not allow them to increase unacknowledged.

Money

Money may be the husk of many things, but not the kernel. It brings you food but not appetite, medicine but not health, acquaintances but not friends, servants but not faithfulness, days of joy but not peace or happiness.

Character

Character is a diamond that surpasses every other stone.

Poverty is uncomfortable, but nine times out of ten, the best thing that can happen to a young man is to be tossed overboard to sink or swim. Taking personal responsibility for our destiny is the stuff character is made of.

Reputation

A good man doubles the length of his existence. To have lived so as to look back with pleasure on our past life is to live twice.

Politics

A liberal is a man who is willing to spend somebody else's money!

Success

The world is divided into people who do things and people who get the credit. Try, if you can, to belong to the first class; there is far less competition.

Relationships

The one who loves the least controls the relationship. Jealousy and possessiveness are signs of insecurity, but they dominate each situation. Therefore, we must break free of these chains we call love, and work on loving ourselves. Only then can we give love to another. Only then will the relationship flourish with neither party controlling or dominating the other.

Seek those who find your road agreeable, your personality and mind stimulating, your philosophy acceptable, and your experience helpful. Let those who do not, seek their own kind.

Knowledge

Three-fourths of the mistakes a man makes are made because he does not really know the things he thinks he knows.

Desire

When you want a thing deeply, honestly, and intensely, this feeling of desire reinforces your will and arouses in you the determination to work for the desired object. When you have a distinct purpose in view, your work becomes of absorbing interest. You bend your best powers to it. You give it concentrated attention. You think of little else than the realization of this purpose. Your will is stimulated into unusual activity and as a consequence, you do your work with an increasing sense of power.

Free Enterprise

Capitalism and communism stand at opposite poles. Their essential difference is this: the communist seeing the rich man and his fine home says, "No man should have so much." The capitalist seeing the same thing says, "All should have this much."

America has achieved its commercial and financial supremacy under a regime of private ownership. It conquered the wilderness; built our railroads, our factories, our utilities; gave us the telegraph, the telephone, the electric light, the automobile, the airplane, the radio, and a higher standard of living for all the people not obtained anywhere else in the world. No great invention ever came from a government-owned industry.

The inherent vice of capitalism is the unequal sharing of blessings while the inherent virtue of socialism is the equal sharing of miseries.

Personal Power

Our personal resources are almost always far greater than we ever imagined them to be. Never ask, Can I do this? Ask, instead, How can I do this?

Success and happiness are reserved and dedicated only to those who feel that better is possible, good is not good enough; to those who believe you can't win if you don't run; to those who know that we should guide by the light of the stars above and not by the light of the ships passing;

and to those who conclude that when you make a dream, it will make you.

I, Doug Davis, teaming up with Samuel Clark, challenge you to accept these philosophies and live by them. The blessing given to me has now been revealed and bestowed upon you. May the "force" be with you always as you weather the storm, and may you stay forever young!

As I finished the last sentence, I went back and reread all the quotes again. Each of them was definitely a capsulized kernel of insight, understanding, and a shining nugget of wisdom. I remembered the old gardener's advice and committed right then and there that I was going to memorize the entire pad. It would take a while, but I was going to do it. The old gardener was right. It's true! We read for enjoyment, but we must memorize for lasting commitment and practical application. I took challenge 3 to heart and took the next few days to study the seventy-five quotes, internalize the information, and commit them all to memory.

The minute I finished with challenge 3 and tested myself on recall, I excitedly turned the page to study challenge 4.

CHALLENGE 4

You are now living the precepts of challenges 1, 2, and 3. You are ready and conditioned now to accept and acknowledge the "power of the dream." Dreams keep things in proper perspective. They remind us that no matter how bad the weather is, or how bad our problems are, each day is a great day. If you don't believe it, try missing just one of them!

Dreams unveil that life is nothing more than a series of choices. Those who learn to make better choices make better lives for themselves, their families, and the ones they love. They think big and become big! They overcome obstacles and always have a reason to get up and go again. Dreams keep our attitude positive, our sense of competition fierce, our stamina strong, our strength powerful, our mental alertness finely tuned, and our lives alive. Yes, dreams will even eliminate suicide and prevent alcohol and drug abuse if we let them.

Dreams are exciting and powerful but only effective when they are realistic. Realistic in that they are obtainable through hard work, practice, preparation, and endurance to the end. That is why when opportunity knocks, make sure you are not in the backyard looking at four-leaf clovers!

Make sure you are ready and willing to go for it by surrounding yourself with others who believe in you and who are also committed to your cause. Let me illustrate the power of a dream and the tremendous influence it can have on others as everyone pitches in to make the dream come true. This is a true story.

Bopsy is a young boy dying of terminal leukemia. At the present time there is absolutely no known cure. One day his mother had the presence of mind to ask him, "Bopsy, if you had one wish and you knew that it would come true, what would you dream about? What would you want?"

Without even thinking about it, Bopsy replied, "Mommy, if I had one dream wish and I knew it would come true, I'd want to be a fireman."

The next morning, Bopsy's mother phoned the local fire department and talked to the fire chief. She explained her son's situation and his wish. The fire chief had a heart as big as a house and answered, "I'd love to make Bopsy's dream come true. You tell him that we will be by to pick him up in the morning at 8:00 a.m. We will make him honorary fire chief for the whole day." The fire chief continued, "If you'll give me Bopsy's measurements, we'll have a helmet made for him just like the big guys wear. We'll have a yellow slicker jacket and rubber galoshes made for him, too."

Sure enough, at 8:00 a.m. the fire engine pulled up in front of Bopsy's house. They helped him get all decked out in his very own fireman's uniform. He got to go out on two fire calls. It inspired him to the depth of his being so that he lived three months longer than any doctor said he could possibly live.

On the last night of Bopsy's short life, the head nurse in the hospital was monitoring his vital signs and saw that they were starting to weaken. Scrambling to help Bopsy in any way she could, the nurse remembered the relationship he had developed with the local fire department.

Immediately she phoned the fire chief and told him, "Bopsy is not doing too good and I thought you would like to know. Maybe there is something you would like to do for him."

The fire chief shouted, "You tell that little guy to hang on. We will be there in five minutes. But, nurse, there are a couple of things we need you to do for us. Will you please announce over the P.A. system of the hospital that everyone is going to hear the sirens screaming and see the lights flashing, and that we are coming to see our boy Bopsy for the last time. And," he continued, "would you please open up the third-story window to Bopsy's hospital room, because this time we are coming in by ladder!"

Moments later the sirens were screaming, the lights were flashing, and the fire engines pulled up in front of the hospital. A huge ladder went up the side of the building. Ten firemen and two firewomen scampered up the ladder and climbed in through the third-story window into Bopsy's hospital room. They kissed him and cuddled him. With tears streaming down everyone's cheeks, the big, burly fire chief leaned over Bopsy's hospital bed and took hold of his frail little hand. Bopsy looked up at the fire chief with a tear in his eye and a big smile on his precious, innocent face. With his last breath, Bopsy asked, "Fire chief, am I now really a fireman?"

The fire chief answered, "Bopsy, you are." And the little guy died.

Can you now see and feel the power of a dream? I believe this story relates to everyone, young and old. Each of us has a dream still stuck inside yet unfulfilled. I challenge you to take time to dig it out and write it down so you can see the dream. Then visualize it, believe in yourself and in the power of the dream and then start immediately to achieve it. Achieve it for yourselves, your families, your country, and for all of mankind. Yes, I challenge you to dream a dream—a good, clean, pure, powerful, positive dream—and make it come true!! As they say here in the

South Pacific, "If you don't have a dream, how are you going to make a dream come true?" If you are presently content with who you are and what you are achieving, make a self-audit. It means you have stopped dreaming, and when you lose your dreams, you die. That's why we have so many people walking around in this world who are already dead and they don't even know it yet. They have stopped dreaming and consequently have stopped changing and improving as disenchanted boredom and uninterested feelings fill their lives.

For this reason, let me once again ask you to reflect on our little boy. Dig deep down inside and uncover that dream wish that each of us has stuck deep down inside still yet unfulfilled. I want you to write it down so that you can "see" it. I want you to start to visualize accomplishing it. Clearly conceive it, believe it, and then go out and achieve it for yourself, for your family, and for all of mankind. Challenge 2 states "You were born to succeed!" Dreaming is the first step in making success a reality. Dreaming helps us live a higher law, honor and respect our families, deal with adversity, and endure to the end to become all that we were truly meant to be. Let me conclude this challenge by solidifying the following four points with illustrations. Why? Stories are great teachers.

Stories Are Great Teachers

I'd rather see a sermon preached than hear one any day,
I'd rather you would walk with me than merely point the way.

Everyone I know likes stories. Therefore, everyone should be able to enjoy life and relate to it. Why do stories intrigue us? Because stories allow us to look at ourselves. They act as mirrors, reflecting our own actions through the actions of others. They make us aware of our own talents or idiosyncrasies and serve as counselors to reward or chastise our behavior in an appropriate, tactful way. They remind us of what Goldsmith said: "People seldom improve when they have no other model but themselves to copy after." The bottom line is that stories pump us up and help us do what is right to make our dreams come true.

Life is nothing more than a collection of what people do and say. When we hear a story about someone else, we immediately think to ourselves, "It happened to him or her, so one day it could happen to me."

We seldom remember statistics, facts, and figures; we seldom forget a good, heart-warming story. Reading a positive story about an experience someone had inspires us to keep life in proper perspective. It reminds us that life really is simple if we make things happen and work to make our dreams come true. Let's see if you agree:

Stride to Be Better

I was in Maui, Hawaii, when Naomi Rhode, a professional speaker, who was also in Hawaii doing seminars, related this experience to me. "My husband and I had been walking along the beach for several hundred yards when I paused to look back to see how far we'd come. I noticed our footprints in the sand and immediately filled with pride. I pointed them out to my husband and commented, 'Wow, think about how many times we have left our footprints in the lives of others.'

"Suddenly the ocean washed in and swept away our footprints, leaving no sign of them ever having been there. I was puzzled and almost hurt. I asked my husband, 'How can we leave a more lasting impression on people that will not be washed away with time?' He wisely replied, 'Just walk on higher ground.'"

Each of us should evaluate our daily life and commit to reaching a higher level of daily living by striving and striding to walk on higher ground.

Honor Your Father and Mother

What does it mean to honor your father and mother? That bit of counsel has been passed down for a few thousand years, so it must be good advice. Honoring your father and your mother was included in the ten items listed in the ten commandments, but how do you do it and why do you do it?

Let me tell you about Leon White, an all-conference linebacker for the BYU Cougars when they were ranked number one in the nation.

At the Holiday Bowl VII in San Diego, Leon White was a one-man wrecking crew. He was all over the football field sacking the quarterback, intercepting passes, and generally becoming a legend in his own time. The crowd loved it. And the informal Leon White fan club went crazy! He was playing better than he had ever played before.

But Leon White wasn't playing for the crowds or for the glory. He was playing for his dad. Leon's dad was terminally ill with cancer and was watching the games from a stretcher on the sidelines. Both of them knew this would be the last game they would share in this life. Between defensive sets, Leon would hustle over and say, "Dad, you having a good time?"

He would answer, "You betcha I am!" And was he ever. Leon's dad never stopped talking about that game and his son, right up until he died a few days later.

Few of us can star in a college bowl game to show our parents how much we appreciate them and how proud we are of them, but that is not the point. Leon's father wasn't proud of him because he was a great linebacker, he was proud because he was a son who made his parents proud.

We can all do that. And when we do, we find that in the eyes of the people who love us most, each of us is all-American.

Miss America

A five-year-old girl wanted to be Miss America. She started to pursue her dream by enrolling in piano lessons, which she continued for fourteen years. She also studied voice lessons for nine years to complete her musical performance package.

Her dream and pursuit of musical excellence came to a screeching halt when she was eleven years old. A serious car accident left her crippled, never to walk again. For ten months she wore a total body cast. When the cast was taken off, she could walk, but only with a severe limp. This added greatly to her mental agony already sustained from the 100 stitches that left a scar on her face.

But she had a dream, so she continued on. At the age of seventeen, through hard work and undying faith, her leg miraculously got better and she tried out for her first county beauty pageant. She lost, not even finishing in the top ten. The next year she entered again and didn't make the five finalists. The third try she won but didn't make the top ten at the state Miss Mississippi Pageant. The fourth year she again won her county contest but again lost by a landslide at the state level. The fifth year, at age 22, her final opportunity to compete before she grew too old, she not only won locally but finally won the state contest and became Miss Mississippi. And at the end of that year, over 75 million television viewers watched teary-eyed Cheryl Pruitt gracefully walk down the runway in Atlantic City to be crowned Miss America.

Was I right? Are you a story fan? I would wager that after reading these stories you are probably committed to living a more exemplary life, hanging in there long enough to make your dreams come true, and spending more time with your loved ones. It is amazing the emotion we can feel in a simple story. We need to know about other people's lives because we can draw inspiration and learn something from everyone.

The Lousy Lawyer

Did you ever totally fail and fall flat on your face? If you haven't, you are different from most of us. So let me tell you about the lousy lawyer.

How could a guy mess up his opportunities much more than this guy did? He came from a wealthy family, he had all the advantages that money and education can give a person, he was the pride of his parents, and had been given the best schooling available. He frittered away most of his time but finally succeeded in getting a law degree. Now what? Now the world was about to look him straight in the eyeball as it does to all of us. Now he couldn't hide behind his father's money or his law degree from a prestigious college or his name or social standing. He was about to enter the courtroom and the judge and jury and particularly his client were only interested in one thing: was he any good as a lawyer?

He wasn't. In fact, he was terrified! He was a flop, a fake, and a failure, and everybody knew it. Worst of all, he knew it! He was too frightened to stand up to the opposition in the courtroom. Embarrassed, he fled to lick his wounds.

But feeling low gave him a view of his fellow human beings he had never seen before. It was a world full of suffering worse than his own. There were other people to consider besides himself, and here was where perhaps even a failure could contribute to the world. .

With these thoughts, the lawyer began crawling out of his shell of self-pity. He never again practiced law, he never stood up and slugged it out with the opposition. Instead he developed his own style of nonviolent protest and with that style led his country, India, to independence and became one of the most powerful world leaders of the century. He became Mahatma Gandhi.

So the next time you're lying flat on your face in failure, look around and see if that position doesn't give you a new perspective. When you're that close to the ground, you may be able to plant some seeds for future success. Among Gandhi's seeds for success is this list of the seven most grievous sins in the world:

1. Wealth without work
2. Pleasure without conscience
3. Knowledge without character
4. Commerce without morality
5. Science without humanity
6. Worship without sacrifice
7. Politics without principle

You, too, can plant some seeds and rise to greatness. You, too, can become all-American to your parents and friends. You, too, can become the Miss or Mister Somebody who is important to you. Therefore, go for it! And live life as if someone is following you around with paper and pen and a camera, recording everything you say and do. You are responsible for what goes into your own story. And when the book of your life is finally released, you can make sure it's something that not only you are proud of, but also an example that others will want to follow. Make it a good, respectable story that others will one day want to tell! Make your life something that inspires others to dream impossible dreams that truly can come true.

I, Grandfather, challenge you to accept this philosophy and live by it. May the "force" be with you always as you weather the storm, and may you stay forever young! End of challenge 4.

So much had happened in my life in the last four days since I found the boomerang and the book that my mind and heart were going at a much more rapid rate than ever before. I needed some time to digest all this information. I decided to take it easy over the weekend. I basically stayed in my bedroom to sleep, read, and sleep some more. My family and friends were concerned about my sudden change in behavior. Most of my friends in high school didn't understand that the choices we make as teenagers will affect us forever. For some reason, we always have a tendency to let life happen to us instead of taking charge and happening to life. There truly is a big difference between growing older and growing up.

After rereading and pondering the quotable quotes in challenge 3 and deeply contemplating challenge 4, the weekend was quickly over. But I was filled with the "force" and left my room more willing and ready to change my life for the better and get on with the new precept in the book. I was finally feeling the "force" acting in my mind and in my heart on a daily basis. Wisdom is usually a gift for the elderly, but the longer I studied Grandfather's philosophies, the wiser I became.

Today was a hot, dry Monday, and I ached for a large chocolate milk shake! School was out so I headed downtown to the mall.

While sitting on a bench slurping down my milk shake, a rude awakening hit me square between my eyes. I noticed for the first time the obstacles, heartaches, handicaps that so many people had to deal with. For so many hours I sat there observing mankind. Wow! Suddenly I didn't seem to have too many problems compared to these brave individuals. I say brave because I could tell they were dealing with their obstacles in a brave, courageous way. They did not let what they could not do interfere with what they could do. And they faced and smiled at every situation with a positive attitude.

One little boy limped out of the men's room. He was only about three years old and was dragging his left foot because of a big steel brace on his left leg. It cut me to the core to see his lameness and embarrassed me deeply to see his energetic life for giving happiness. I felt guilty for all the times I had complained about a headache or a sore back. The times I had sprained my ankle or broken up with my girlfriend that were such big problems then now seemed so trivial compared to what this little guy was dealing with for the rest of his life. Perspective? What a difference the right one makes in living life to its fullest.

That day in the mall I also saw a young man by the name of Alvin Law playing the drums. Alvin is from Canada and is the best drummer I had ever heard. His drumming is incredible, but more incredible is the fact that he was born with no arms. Alvin played a ten-minute drum solo by holding the drumsticks with his feet. Alvin is also an accomplished musician on the trombone, a pretty good typist, and has great handwriting (footwriting!). He does everything people with hands can do: he eats at the table, holds his glass to drink, etc.

I also met Roger Crawford in the mall and listened to him speak. What a wonderful day I had. Crawford is one of the very best motivational speakers and corporate consultants in the world. Roger Crawford was born with one finger on his right hand, two fingers on his left hand, no left leg, and two toes on his right foot. Yet, Roger played division I mens' tennis on the Loyola Marimount University tennis team while attending college there and graduated one of the top in his class. Roger's win/loss record as a tennis player (which, incidentally, he achieved playing the top players in the USA) was forty-six wins, seven losses. At the mall they showed a videotape of him playing. Amazingly, he played with a Wilson A2A tennis racket and every shot was a two-handed effort.

I finished my milk shake and started for home. As I was leaving the mall, I passed by a cute little girl strapped in a wheelchair. At a closer glance, I saw a group of ten kids all in wheelchairs. Each of them had cerebral palsy. As I got closer I noticed five other kids standing in the corner. Each was severely mentally handicapped in some way. None of the kids in or out of the wheelchairs could talk. My heart went out to them as I exited through the doors out onto the street. During the walk home I thought to myself, "I don't have any problems or challenges compared to those individuals. Who was I fooling complaining about the little things that happened to me?" Suddenly my family life was thrown into a better perspective. I realized how lucky I was to have brothers and a sister who could talk to me, even argue and throw things at me if they wanted to! Obstacles are really no big deal if we face them head on and address them when they occur. Obstacles are no big deal if we choose to not let what we can not do interfere with what we can do. For the longer we wait to deal with our challenges, the bigger they get and the more we want to complain, feel sorry for ourselves, and label them unsolvable.

I arrived home and immediately locked myself in my room so I could continue to read Grandfather's challenges. As I pondered my day at the mall, I opened my sacred book and turned to the page marked challenge 5.

CHALLENGE 5

Obstacles Can Be Steppingstones

"We cannot direct the wind—but we can adjust the sails. Nothing will ever be attempted if all possible objections must first be overcome."

When I was in Las Vegas, Nevada, watching a professional tennis match between Jimmy Connors and another top-ranked player, Connors was winning because his opponent continually hit the ball into the net. After awhile, a frustrated woman sitting behind me yelled out, "Why don't they just take down the stupid net!"

How many of us wake up each morning silently yelling the same thing, hoping that our day will be void of obstacles and that we won't have any "nets" to contend with?

Even though this would make our lives easier, we don't really want a carefree life. We would never grow through overcoming obstacles. "The brook loses its music when you remove the rocks." W.M. Lewis said, "The tragedy of life is not that it ends so soon, but that we wait so long to begin it."

It takes courage to push yourself to places where you have never been before—to test your limits—to break through barriers. But it's these barriers or obstacles that force us to stop procrastinating and do something now. Adversity causes some men to break but others to break records! Therefore, our primary purpose is to become expert problem solvers. Oliver Wendell Holmes said, "The greatest thing in this world is not so much where we are, but in what direction we are moving." This does not involve taking crazy, uncalculated risks that cause unnecessary problems in our lives, but, instead, facing systematic problems that occur and turning them into challenges that allow us to grow and progress. The idea is to turn our lemons into lemonade! Henry Kaiser said, "I always view problems as opportunities in work clothes." Turning your back on one problem brings you face to face with another. So don't avoid them! Grow from obstacles and learn from mistakes and successes of others; you won't live long enough to make them all yourself. Remember, a path with no obstacles probably leads nowhere. Success is measured not by substance obtained, but by obstacles overcome.

It's Gonna Hurt

The next time you're faced with something difficult, grit your teeth and get through it because there is always something good on the other side. There's a storm before the rainbow, sorrow before joy. My coach used to say, "No pain, no gain!" Many of life's failures are men and women who did not realize how close they were to success when they gave up! Therefore, we need to remember, the thing to try when all else fails is again! To succeed is to do the best you can, where you are, with what you have. Overcoming obstacles and rising each time we fall, then, are critical ingredients to becoming successful and winning.

A friend of mine from Canada is a high-school basketball coach. He inherited a team that had not won a game in four years. During his first year as coach, his team experienced tremendous obstacles and won only four games. Was he a winner? Were his players winners? Sure, they lost eleven games and ran into most of their obstacles, but they won four more than they ever had before. Yes, indeed, they were winners! The object in winning is not to defeat your opponent, but rather to better your own past best personal performance, and that's just what this team did.

When dealing with obstacles, whether it's a game, a schoolroom, a business transaction, or anything else in between, we should pause afterward and answer the following four questions:

1. What did I do well?
2. What did the team (or business organization or students or family) do well?
3. What can I improve upon?
4. What can the team (or business organization or students or family) improve upon?

Think about the importance of having everyday obstacles to overcome. It's out of obstacles that these four questions about growth and self-improvement spring.

If we're not failing a few times it means we're not pushing ourselves hard enough. It's okay, blow it! We're only human—we're supposed to make mistakes. But make a different one each time. A mistake is evidence that at least something was attempted. A mistake duplicated is evidence of an immature idiot!

As we now plunge deeper, remember something: obstacles are those scary things you see when you take your eyes off your goal. But if used right, they can help you rise to your ultimate capacity as a human being. Winston Churchill said, "Kites rise highest against the wind, not with it." Behold the turtle: it makes progress only when it sticks its neck out. Go for it full speed ahead and don't worry about losing. Be determined to win; do your very, very best and let what happens, happen. Let me explain how this philosophy works by relating four illustrations.

A Swimmer's Glory

Michael Swenson loved to swim. In fact, every night after school he would go to the community pool and swim lap after lap just for pure enjoyment. As time went on, Michael reached the age when he really needed some attention and recognition. And how do we get recognition? Usually by doing something we are good at doing. In Michael's case, he decided to enter a swimming meet. Ironically, the following day an ad appeared in the newspaper announcing a local swimming race. Michael entered and continued to practice. It was a ten-mile race across a lake and with only four weeks to prepare, Michael intensified his workouts.

Race day finally came, and to Michael's astonishment, hundreds of contestants had entered. On top of this pressure, entire outlying communities of thousands of people showed up to cheer on their favorite contestants.

Instructions were given, the swimmers were lined up, and—pow!—the gun went off to start the race. Michael's preparation and hard work paid off. At the five-mile mark he had a commanding lead. But then temptation struck. Fatigue turned Michael into a coward as he gave in to negative thoughts such as: What am I trying to prove? I can't make it; I'll quit now but learn from this so I can win next time.

As Michael became fatigued, the second-place swimmer started to make his move. He swam to within one hundred yards of Michael at the eight-mile mark, but Michael fought back. He was able to put the negative thoughts aside and push himself to greatness. He wanted this victory, this glory.

At the nine-mile mark, the second-place swimmer was now only thirty yards behind Michael. Michael knew it and pushed and pulled even harder. But wouldn't you know it. With only five yards to go, the second place swimmer passed Michael and won the race. Both swimmers collapsed from total exhaustion and lay down on the sand. Then something interesting happened. Sure, all the spectators congratulated the winner of the race for his excellence, but immediately after that their attention turned to Michael. Why? Michael was confused. He didn't win. A lady who didn't see the race but was at the finish line also was confused. She couldn't see Michael but did know that he had only taken second. She tapped a man on the shoulder and inquired, "Why are they making such a big deal out of him? He didn't win!"

The man turned to her and replied, "Because Michael would have easily won had he had two arms!"

Learn from Others

In 1965, a championship game was being played between two of America's finest high-school basketball teams. DeMatha Prep of Hyattsville, Maryland, was playing against undefeated Power Memorial from New York City. Power had a seventy-one-game winning streak coming into the game. DeMatha's only chance of defeating Power was if they stopped Power's 7' 1" center, Lew Alcindor. DeMatha put its two biggest men on Alcindor and the strategy worked; they won, 46 to 43.

The loss was Alcindor's first since he was a high-school freshman. It popped a dream and ended a nationally recognized seventy-one-game win streak. He was heartbroken about the loss but got over it in a few hours. When interviewed, Lew Alcindor taught us something invaluable. "Anybody can lose," he explained, "The idea is to make losing a novelty, not a bad habit." He practices what he preaches as he now has become the greatest center ever to play college or professional basketball. He has since changed his name to Kareem Abdul Jabbar and proves to everyone that the world is not interested in the storms you encountered, but what you brought in the ship.

From Bottom to Top with Determination

Henry Aaron broke Babe Ruth's career home run record of 714 and became the greatest long-ball hitter in baseball history. He now holds the record for the most career homers. Henry didn't start at the top. He didn't play baseball in high school because his school didn't have a team. Besides, he preferred to read. It wasn't until he was in his early twenties that Aaron finally caught baseball fever and decided he wanted to pursue professional sports. His first experience came as a member of a semi-pro team called the Indianapolis Clowns of the Negro American League. This was at a time when there were few blacks playing in the major leagues.

Henry played for $200 a month, hoping and waiting for his chance until he got a break. At last, it came. The scout for the Atlanta Braves spotted him and called him up to the big time. When Henry came up to bat for the first time in his major league career, he was understandably nervous. Thousands of fans were watching, there were two outs, and the pressure was on him to perform. To cap it off, the opposing team's catcher sneered at Henry as he came to the plate. He noticed that Henry batted with a cross-handed grip and made fun of him saying, "Hey, kid, you're holding the bat wrong. You're supposed to hold it so you can read the label."

Henry turned and looked straight into the catcher's eyes. "I didn't come here to read," he said, "I came here to hit." With that he drilled the next pitch into the outfield for a single and giggled all the way to first base.

Henry Aaron went on to play professional baseball for years and holds most of the batting records to date. He understands the saying, "Believe in yourself; at times you're the only one who will."

Back to the Basics for Victory

Billy Casper is one of the greatest golfers of all time. Besides that, he is a dear friend of mine and one of my idols. Why is he my idol? His story sets an example of excellence for the world to follow.

As soon as Billy was big enough to swing a club, his dad started giving him golf lessons. By the time he was fifteen years old he was captain of his high-school team.

He won the San Diego County California Amateurs and Open Championships and turned pro at nineteen. Once Billy became a professional in 1955, financial success came quickly. He was one of the first two men ever to win one million dollars playing golf and only the second golfer in history to win $200,000 in one year. He was named Golfer of the Year on several occasions and for many years led all other golfers on the professional tour in lowest average score, fewest bogies, and fewest putts per hole. In the 1960s Casper was golf's greatest and most consistent performer. He was among the top five money winners every year for over a decade.

The story that typifies Billy's unbelievable ability to concentrate and perform while dealing with obstacles took place during the 1966 U.S. Open at the Olympic Club in San Francisco. Billy had won the U.S. Open in 1959 at the age of twenty-nine—the youngest man to win the Open in twenty years. Now he had an opportunity to win again. No one else gave him a chance, but he wanted to prove that he could win. He had been in a slump for several months.

Going into the last nine holes of the final round, Casper trailed Arnold Palmer by seven strokes. "Impossible," they all said. But Casper shot an amazing 32 on the last nine, Palmer shot 39, and they tied for the championship after regulation play. In an eighteen-hole playoff the next day, Casper fell behind by two strokes after the front nine holes. But he hung in there, kept believing in himself and in his ability, and overtook Palmer again, shooting a 69 and winning by four shots. Billy had won his second U.S. Open championship! Billy Casper understands that when things start going wrong and you feel like the wheels are falling off of your wagon, go back to the basics. Master the fundamentals and you'll eventually win again and again.

These four great sports heroes are like heroes in all walks of life. They all share a common denominator and fully comprehend the words of William Jennings Bryan: "Destiny is not a matter of chance, it is a matter of choice; it is not a thing to be waited for, it is a thing to be achieved." Bryan doesn't expect to find life worth living—he makes it that way! We should, too!

I, Grandfather, challenge you to accept this philosophy and live by it! May the "force" be with you always as you weather the storm, and may you stay forever young. End of challenge 5.

Challenge 5 served me well. It was inspirational, which moved me into greater personal self-motivation to become the very best I could be. I reread it several times to internalize the message and ensure a long-term effect. I fell asleep late that night and woke up the next morning with a whole new, refreshing, positive outlook on living. When my alarm clock went off, I didn't get ticked off! I realized you can't make your dreams come true by oversleeping! My alarm clock was suddenly an "opportunity clock." I looked out my window and saw a street light in the distance. I realized it wasn't a stop light (which is negative), it was a "Go" light. The radio weather report blurted out "70 percent chance of rain," and I immediately thought, "All right, today there is a 30 percent chance—a 3 in 10 chance for sunshine!" Sure, every rose has its thorns, but why not look for the flower instead of the thistle?

Today I realized that for the first time in my life I was in control of my thinking, my actions, and my life. I felt powerful! Positive thinking really does make a difference. I have heard for years about the word *motivation*. Leaders always say, "You've got to be motivated!" After all this time, I finally wanted to know what it meant. I excitedly opened up the sacred book and turned to read and study challenge 6.

CHALLENGE 6

Motivation—Goal Setting
Needing, Loving, Winning

Knute Rockne said, "An automobile goes nowhere efficiently unless it has a quick, hot spark to ignite things, to set the cogs of the machine in motion. So I try to make every player on my team feel needed—that he's the spark keeping our machine in motion. On him depends our success."

We have mentioned the importance of positive thinking as it affects our performance and health. We have mentioned the importance of changing our attitude and actions to accomplish our goals. But we have yet to discuss how to sustain this change. Some people may think it's George Orwell's 1984 come true. But it is clearly a step beyond that.

When Orwell wrote his book on a society ruled by manipulation of the mind in the mythical year 1984, I'm sure he didn't imagine that by the real year 1984 people would be willing not only to have their subconscious minds manipulated but would pay for it and purchase books, audiotapes and videotapes to change the way they think and feel.

Yes, we finally have discovered that success is a step-by-step process that requires step-by-step motivation both from within and from outward stimulation.

Vince Lombardi said, "The difference between a successful person and others is not a lack of strength, not a lack of knowledge, but rather in a lack of will." Lombardi also said, "Coaches who can outline plays on a chalkboard are a dime a dozen. The ones who win get inside each player and inspire!" H. E. Jansen said, "The man who wins may have been counted out several times, but he didn't hear the referee." Remember, in great attempts it is glorious even to fail. Alex Haley, author of *Roots,* wrote seven nights a week for eight years before he sold his first magazine article for $100. During that time he accumulated a debt of $100,000. Pittsburgh Steeler Quarterback Terry Bradshaw won four Super Bowl championships. He did not make his school team the first time he tried out. Robert Kennedy lost the election for class president in college. Einstein flunked mathematics. President Roosevelt's wife and mother both died on the same night.

Can you see the importance of motivation? Sustaining motivation is the key to dealing with stress, overcoming obstacles, and achieving success!

Needs, Motivators—Understanding, Satisfying

Let's discuss motivation as a way to satisfy our individual needs. Each of us, regardless of our age, interests, race, color, sex, or ability, has the inherent urge to satisfy three basic needs:

1. The need to feel love
2. The need to feel wanted and important
3. The need to feel a true sense of security

Because this urge to satisfy these needs is so strong, we will do anything to fulfill them. We will change our hairstyles, our vocabulary, our clothing, our health codes, our environment, our friends, and even our moral standards just to satisfy these needs. It's scary, but it's true! These three needs control our subconscious efforts to satisfy all other needs.

Ask yourself, "What am I doing or not doing on a daily basis to satisfy these fundamental needs in my life?" In the process, are you compromising your values and principles?

As we attempt to fulfill our needs, the question of motivation arises. There are five basic motivators that influence us to do something:

1. Necessity (food, clothing, shelter)
2. Luxury (fine food, expensive clothes, big house, automobile, TV, VCR, expensive vacations)
3. Power (to delegate, be the boss, make the decisions, get your own way)
4. Recognition (look at me—I did that, I'm as good as you; good job—keep up the good work)
5. Service to your fellow men

Research indicates that the first four motivators don't make one happy without the fifth. Every individual needs to believe that he or she is making a significant contribution. What it boils down to is service seems to be the most important motivator of all!

Again, ask yourself, How are these motivators affecting my priorities and goal direction? How am I satisfying my three basic needs of love, importance, and security in my work and play?

To answer correctly, we must examine motivation by itself. What is motivation? Broken down it means "a motive for action." It means we are not only fired up and excited for the moment, we are also leaving the meeting or situation having accomplished something. It means we are feeling pumped up to succeed, but that we are also looking forward to doing something in the near future with a specific direction and goal. It means we are committed to changing ourselves first and then committed in heart and soul to teaching others what we've learned. Motivation isn't instant—it's a process!

Motivation is the life blood of every action, but it will do us absolutely no good at all if all we are is a motivated mass of indirection! We must funnel this developed energy into a meaningful, specific, tangible purpose called *goal setting.*

Simple Steps to Goal Setting

Have a dream. Make it big but feasible. Make sure it is your dream and not someone else's. It must be important to you so it can become an obsession to achieve. You must understand that the end result is a definite bargain in exchange for the effort you will make.

Set yourself a realistic deadline for completion. (Not *I will lose 1,500 pounds by Friday.*) Be honest and reasonable but still push yourself to a finish date that will make you work, stretch, push, sacrifice, and maintain your enthusiasm.

Back off to gain perspective to see where you are now and where it is that you want to be. This allows you the insight and the foresight to plan out the step-by-step process that you must strictly follow in order to cover all the losses and make your dream come true on time.

Set goals. Goals are the tools we use to make our dreams come true. But remember, goals are only an excuse for the game. Long-range, medium-range, and short-range goals are all important; especially the short-range daily/hourly goals! They must be clearly defined and measurable. Break time down into increments of months, weeks, days, hours, and specific blocks of time. This allows us to always know where we are, how far we have come, and how far we still need to go. Short-range goals are most important because they give us checkpoints to examine our progress by. They help us play and enjoy the game in-between the long-range goals! This sustains our motivation as we see ourselves getting closer to the big goal and making our dream come true.

Do it now! Start today! The hardest step is always the first! Get it over with as soon as possible. Believe you can do it and do it!

Elementary Example

I want to read a book. It is *my* choice. I am excited! I want to have it completed in thirty days.

The book has 450 pages (how will I ever finish it?).

I read twenty pages an hour at a comfortable pace with good understanding and retention level.

There are 450 pages in this "long book," so I will divide the number of pages I read per hour into the total number of pages in the book.

This equals twenty-two-and-a-half hours of reading.

To accomplish my goal in the thirty-day time limit, I prepare a daily schedule and fill in my "fixed times" (work, school, etc.). This allows me to calculate my "flexible time" and itemize each day into hours available to read.

The last step is to simply plug the required twenty-two-and-a-half hours of reading time into the available flexible time.

If there isn't enough flexible time, create more of it by waking up earlier in the morning, reading during meals, sacrificing a social event, or piling up the reading time on the weekends.

The key to successful dreaming and goal setting is to truly want to accomplish the goal to the degree that you will be willing to do what you need to do to get the job done. This is what is meant by motivation. Motivation means nothing unless it accompanies specific, meaningful, predetermined, action-oriented goals. We must always have a "reason to succeed!"

Kinds of Motivation

We are exposed to three forms of motivation on a daily basis:

1. Fear Motivation (Do it or else.)
2. Reward Motivation (Do it for a prize.)
3. Self-Motivation (Do it because *you* want to do it.).

Fear motivation works only on the outside. It's superficial. In athletics, fear gets players to run only when the coach is watching. And it's what an athlete does when the coach isn't around that makes him or her a champion! At home, children go to bed only when their parents are there to enforce the rules. At school, students under fear concentrate on getting away with things without getting into trouble instead of concentrating on learning. They do just enough work to get by. Fear motivation gets us to go only through the motions. Our heart is not in the task. We are simply trying to please someone else. Fear motivation only confuses activity with accomplishment!

Reward motivation works only if the prize has been decided upon by the person expected to win it. If the reward does not interest the individual, there will be no motivation. Some students aren't motivated by As and Bs. Some teachers aren't motivated by money. Some salespersons aren't motivated by a vacation to the Bahamas. Reward motivation used ineffectively also causes confusion between activity and accomplishment. It also gets us to go only through the motions. How many persons do you know who are reward-motivated by the retirement pension plan and by the supposed security of a union or government job, and only go through work motions and put in their time? Even though they come to work they are virtually dead, and, through their lack of motivation and lack of conscientiousness, they are literally "killing" fellow workers and friends as well. This is the perfect example of the aforementioned statement, *some confuse activity with accomplishment.*

If fear and reward motivation do not stimulate us to do our best, then self-motivation must be the key. Self-motivation is operative when we complete a task because we want to get it done, not because someone is forcing or bribing us to do so. Our whole heart and soul are committed to the accomplishment. It's like the story of the pig and the chicken. They are walking down a road when they see a sign that advertises: Ham and Eggs Breakfast Special! The chicken says, "Wow, that sounds great." The pig replies, "That's easy for you to say. You only have to participate; I must make a total commitment!" When we're self-motivated we gladly go to work early and stay late to get the job done—in school, in sports, in music, in life! Self-motivation spawns personal discipline and total commitment to a cause.

Self-Motivation—The Ultimate Key!

To be Self-Motivated we need to honestly answer these three questions:

1. Why should I?
2. What's in it for me?
3. Will it make me feel wanted and important?

If we can answer these questions, we will be able to commit ourselves to our cause and go for it. The motivation will be sustained from within and will not waver when the trials and tribulations come. Self-motivation will prove the statement "You can if *you* think you can" true. It will sustain us through times of trouble and keep us aware that the end result is a definite bargain.

As we have listed the three basic needs of every individual, the five motivators, and the three kinds of motivation, I draw your attention to the repeated phrase *wanted and important.* It is a part of every phase of motivation. In fact, all of our needs are secondary to satisfying our feeling that we are needed, that we belong.

I Love You, I Need You

Psychologists proclaim that the three most powerful and moving words in the world are *I love you.* I never gave it much thought—but now I disagree! The three most powerful, moving, important words are, *I need you.* If we say "I love you," we must reinforce it with action that proves we need the one we love. I realize philosophers and religious books state the importance of love. But they also state, "If ye love me, keep my commandments." We need to show our love through sincere action.

Example 1

Little Johnny is playing catch in the front yard with a baseball and glove. As he throws the ball up and catches it, his father arrives home from work. As his father gets out of his car, Johnny excitedly asks, "Dad, will you play ball with me?"

His father replies, "Johnny, I have a lot of work to do so I don't have time. But I want you to know that I love you."

Johnny counters, "Dad, I don't want you to love me, I want you to play ball with me!"

The need to feel needed and wanted and important overshadows the need to be loved. This previous story demonstrates that any male can be a father, but it takes a special man to be a dad! Being a real dad takes Time!!

Example 2

I am a musician. I like to sing and have written some songs. I got my start writing music when a friend of mine called and asked me to write a song for his wedding. A couple of days later he called back and said the band had canceled and would I take its place? I agreed and practiced about twenty songs to play at the reception. At the wedding I played the love song I had written and continued with my program. After two songs the band showed up and wanted to perform. There had been a miscommunication in the party planning. I'm easygoing, so I helped the band set up. Besides, it's more fun to eat and mingle at a wedding reception than to sing. I ate some cake, stayed for about thirty minutes, then packed up my guitar and went home.

Here is the key to the story. My friend Jeff *loved* me and he knew that I *loved* him. That's not the reason why I consented to fill in for the band. Jeff *needed* me, and because he *needed* me I willingly did what I could do. If he had *needed* me to help in the kitchen or had *needed* me to wait tables, do the dishes, or clean up, I would have stayed until 3:30 in the morning. But because Jeff no longer *needed* me when the band showed up I left. Sure, Jeff loved me, but that was not enough to keep me at the wedding.

Example 3

I was speaking to the group called Our Primary Purpose, a highly acclaimed program for chemically dependent teenagers in Des Moines, Iowa. At the third meeting that day, one just for parents, a mother shared this story when I explained my "I need you" theory.

Her twenty-year-old son John, who incidentally was not enrolled in the OPP program, was handsome, talented, a good citizen, a good student, a good musician, a good athlete. He also had a lovely girlfriend and seemingly no problems. One day he stopped talking as much as he usually did. Thirty days passed and his conversation dwindled to nothing. He was depressed and his parents and girlfriend continually told him they loved him. He knew they loved him and he expressed his love for them. Everyone was concerned about his well-being and wondered what they could say or do to help him. "I love you" wasn't helping the situation.

John finally made a move. He locked himself in the basement cellar. He was down in the dim dampness for three days, without food, just moping in self pity. Sure he acknowledged his parents love for him and his love for them. But his depression deepened and his loved ones were convinced suicide was imminent. They felt powerless to help John. Even his girlfriend's pleas of love and concern failed.

On the third day of John's isolation, the local high-school football coach, who, incidentally, didn't know what was going on in John's life, called his home to talk to him. John's mother said John was busy and took a message at the coach's request. Then she went to the door of the cellar and called down the stairs. "John, Coach Ivers just phoned. He said that his players voted last night on who they wanted as their assistant coach. They said you were the greatest little league coach they had ever had, and they think they can win the state championship if you help coach them. Coach Ivers says they need you—he needs you! He says if you're interested you should be at football practice at 2:45 this afternoon."

Do you know what happened? Sure you do! John came out of the cellar and went to practice. He accepted the coaching job and when he came home from his first practice, he had snapped out of his depression. He once again felt needed and wanted and important and was back to his old self.

Before we have to experience an ordeal like John did, let us take some preventive measures to ensure lasting feelings of self-worth. Satisfying our need to feel needed is important. And the responsibility is on our own shoulders. We can't afford to wait for someone else to tell us or show us we are needed. We must take pride and personal responsibility to prove it to ourselves on a daily basis. And the way we prove that we're needed? Through participation! Yes, we need to get involved. We become needed as we participate more in our families, schools, jobs, and communities. In fact, as we participate we become better at what we do and eventually become winners!

It's true. Satisfying our need to feel needed allows us to become winners and winning is what we celebrate. Everyone likes to do business with a winner. Therefore, the best way to satisfy all our needs for direction, motivation and feelings of worth is to focus on winning. And when you truly understand it, winning isn't everything—it's the only thing! People say, "It's not whether you win or lose, but how you play the game." Wrong! Why in the heck do we keep score?!

Duffy Daugherty, Michigan State football coach, explains winning this way: "When you're playing for the national championship, it's not a matter of life or death. It's more important than that!" An anonymous alumnus sent a telegram to the football coach that read, "Remember, Coach, we're all behind you—win or tie." Ray Malavasi, former coach of the L.A. Rams, adds, "They say losing builds character. I have all the character I need. I need to win!"

A dear friend of mine, Normand Gibbons, wrote an essay on winning. It is one of the best I've read and truly explains the essence of what it means to be a real winner. Because winning is important to motivation, I share this essay with you!

> I'd like to talk with you about the choice that "makes the difference"—the choice to be a winner.
>
> I'll start by submitting that to win is not to defeat another person. Rather, genuine winning is a process of becoming and enhancing yourself. It is tragically common to see persons who are winners in the first definition—those who have consistently beaten their competitors and have amassed a number of the modern symbols of fortune . . . have lives that are wrenched with disappointment and despair. Too many of these "winners" turn their backs on living altogether. We can all think of prominent, tragic examples. What, then, is the difference between

these desperate souls and the winners who find joy and satisfaction in the success? James and Joneward, two prominent California therapists, describe winning as being a matter of daring to seek a more genuine success. They say, "It takes courage to be a real winner—not a winner in the sense of beating out the other guy by always insisting on winning over him—but winning at responding to life. It takes courage to experience the freedom that comes from autonomy, courage to accept intimacy and directly encounter other persons, courage to take a stand on an unpopular cause, courage to choose authenticity over approval and to choose it again and again, courage to accept the responsibility of your own choices, and, indeed, courage to be the very unique person you really are."

It would seem, then, that being a winner is being real, choosing genuine value over a hollow show or a quest to make an impression. It means daring to give the world who you really are and not the mannikin copy it often seems to expect. In the decisions you will be making . . . to design a life you will be pleased with, the choice between really winning and just appearing to win will be faced again and again.

> The error of the ages
> Why so many do not win
> Is always seeking power without
> Instead of power within.

I considered and decided that the element I see as most important to decide upon in becoming a lifetime, genuine winner, a winner from within, is Authenticity.

To be satisfied and joyful with success, it must be your success—you must win through Authenticity. If in your quest for accomplishment or acceptance you stop being who you really are, then whatever plaudits come your way will be intended for the person you are pretending to be. It can hardly be of value to be rewarded for not being you. The real person you are will be looking outward from the prison you will have fashioned from affectation and sham, and you will feel more and more lonely and unacceptable. Whatever success you seek, let it come from expressing the best of who you are, and it will be a success of worth.

The story is told of a religious leader who lived his entire life inauthentically. He sought honors and accomplishments and won many of them, but as he neared his death, he looked back on his life with regret. "Why are you sad?" asked one of his close friends. "Your life has been successful." The man answered sadly, "I am about to die. Soon I will answer for my life. When that comes, I will not be asked why I was not Moses. I will be asked why I was not myself." Likewise, the greatness which awaits you in your life does not demand that you be Moses, or an Einstein or anyone but you. If you can make that authentic choice—the choice to be yourself, honestly, you will discover more treasure within than you ever imagined. Your life will discover its own purpose—a purpose you may not yet have even considered. In the life of Gandhi, we watched a man discover greatness by continually discovering and expressing his best and most honest self. He was so consistent in his authenticity that he could say without reservation, "My life is my message." He truly was a winner and you can be too!

To win, then, means to be the best you can be. When you are, you become needed as a pillar of strength and leadership to those around you. Suddenly you start to participate more and start to give back to society. This equates to love. As you love, you receive love in return. "What Goes Around Comes Around!" As you receive love, you satisfy your needs to feel wanted and secure. Now all three needs have been met and you're on your way to true happiness and winning.

Winning truly does get us to unveil our true selves and become the best we can be. And when we discover ourselves and like what we find, it's easy to sustain motivation and maintain individuality. Motivation and Individuality are inseparable. One sustains the other.

Individuality: The Key to Living with Yourself

Mark Twain said, "Don't try to teach a pig to sing. It's a waste of your time, and it annoys the pig." One of the things Twain is saying here is that it's important to maintain our individuality. This is one of the most difficult tasks facing mankind today. We see so many gorgeous, glamorous, famous stars in the movies and on TV and the green monster of envy rears its ugly head. "If only I could look like her, if only I could run like him or sing like them," we say. We always want to be like someone else, or at least we think we do. But satisfaction with oneself can be even more fulfilling than copying an entertainer. We need to look within ourselves, discover who we are, and work on becoming aware of and maintaining one of our most important facets: our self-identity. Self-identity and self-awareness equal individuality, and that's what makes each of us special in our potential to contribute meaningfully to our world. Once we have reached this level of understanding, maintaining individuality includes respecting others—their property, their talents, and their goals. It involves respecting their wants and feelings instead of trying to impose our wants and feelings upon them.

Children Belong to Tomorrow

Kahil Gibran wrote, "Your children (or future children) are not your children. They are sons and daughters of life's longing for itself. They come through you but they do not come from you. And though they are with you, they belong not to you. You may give them your love, but not always your thoughts, for they have their own thoughts. You may house their bodies but not their souls. Their souls dwell in the house of their tomorrow, which you cannot visit—not even in your dreams. You may strive to be like them, but seek not to make them be like you. Life goes not backward or tarries with yesterday." I trust this short statement of truth about individuality will be self-explanatory.

The story of respecting individuality and friendship is not the outstretched hand, the kindly smile, or the joy of companionship. It is the joy that comes when someone discovers that someone else believes in him and is willing to trust him. "If it were not for hopes, the heart would break." True! But they must be my hopes for me and your hopes for you. The greatest good that you can do for another is not just to share with him your riches, but to reveal to him his own. Who we are and who we become is determined by those who love us, but those who love us and those we love must retain their own identity. Good relationships involve not only finding the right person, but being the right person. Love endures only if the lovers love many things together and not merely each other. And these "many things" are first developed on our own before we team up with someone to share them with. By searching our souls to find our interests, desires, and directions, we open uncountable doors for lasting relationships to develop the kind that are based on real people instead of fantasy people.

Everything we ever hope to be rests on this fundamental principle of authentic self-discovery and maintaining our individuality. Therefore, as we stick to our guns we must realize that "a friend is someone who knows you as you are, understands who you've been, accepts who you've become, and still gently invites you to grow." And when it's our turn, we must do the same. Yes, opportunity growth, where we help others to grow, is one of the keys to maintaining individuality. And the best way to help others to grow is to help them help themselves. Remember the familiar saying, "Give a man a fish and he'll live for a day. Teach him to fish and he'll live forever."

Support: In Good Times or Bad Times?

Maintaining individuality is a sign of maturity. It implies that we know how to share in another's success. Did you ever notice that we offer great support when others are suffering? We rally around people when they're down. However, we rarely show the same empathy when good things happen to people, especially to those we know fairly well. How many times does a job promotion, an exciting award, or a free trip cause a bit of envy to come over you when a friend is the recipient?

Envy is a sign of insecurity and it stifles our individuality. Coveting our neighbor's goods or successes is to break one of the Ten Commandments! It's definitely a characteristic we don't want or need. Envy comes as we question our own abilities. We become stale in our goal setting and stagnant in our personal growth. The way we eliminate this envy from our lives is to maintain our individual goals, dreams, and desires. This in turn maintains our self-motivation to become the best we can possibly be!

As we maintain our individuality, we learn another important survival skill that helps us to better interact with people. "You can easily judge the character of a man by how he treats those who can do nothing for him." Most of us get so caught up in our own lives that we seldom stop to help another who is in need. We don't want to get involved. Why not? Are we afraid of what may happen as a result of our involvement, or do we rationalize our way out of helping because we're in a hurry and don't have time? We think someone else will always come to the rescue. Read and ponder the following story:

Blind Man's Dog Killed: No One Helped

New York—Joel Shulman never felt so alone and terrified in his life. "I could feel the chain links of her leash slipping through my fingers, but there was nothing I could do."

Shulman, a blind jazz pianist, stood on a subway platform Sunday night and, as his Seeing-Eye dog fell onto the tracks, could only cry out, "Bess, Bess, come on up here, girl."

A second later, the seventeen-year-old Labrador retriever was crushed beneath the wheels of a subway train.

"As the train got closer, I could feel the momentum of the approaching cars and I knew there was nothing I could do," Shulman recalled. "There was no way I could stop the train."

Shulman called out for help from the people around him on the platform, but no one responded.

"The people on that platform saw it all happen and not one of them took ten minutes of his or her time to help; not one was willing to wait for the next train. Not one answered when I called out. Everyone had gotten on the train to go their own ways."

Suddenly Shulman realized he was alone on the platform. "I shook all over as I called and reached out for someone to help, but there was no one there."

Slowly he managed to inch his way back up the subway stairs.

Shulman didn't go to work that night. He stayed home to mourn "the most gentle and affectionate animal I ever knew."

Ask yourself if you would help someone who couldn't get you a starting position, a better job, a fancier car, or an elected office? Would you stop a fight, put out a fire, administer first aid? Those who maintain a positive self-image and their individuality would definitely come to the rescue! Read and ponder again:

Hundreds Watched Man Bleed

Chicago—Charlie Flowers, 39, is alive today, thanks to a Chicago high school principal, and no thanks to several hundred others who ignored his plight.

Principal James Maloney found Flowers bleeding on the street near Crane High School after a student rushed into his office and told him a man outside was hurt.

"I didn't know what it might be," Maloney said. "Was he one of my students, that's all I could think.

"I ran across the street to find a man lying there; I'd never seen so much blood. Just looking at the fellow, it was obvious he couldn't last long unless the bleeding was stopped. He had cuts on his arms, throat, face, and head. The head wound was the worst. Blood was spurting out of a spot near his left temple."

Yet, until Maloney had come to his aid, cars had driven around Flowers while several hundred persons just stood by and watched.

"I remembered something I learned in college about how to stop severe bleeding. I got a handkerchief, put pressure on the wound, and yelled for someone to call the police.

"It must have been about ten minutes that I helped him, all the time trying to keep him quiet, because every time he moved, the bleeding would get worse."

Finally the police and an ambulance arrived and Flowers was taken to a hospital where he underwent surgery and eventually recovered.

Police said he'd been struck on the head by a lead pipe and then stabbed half a dozen times. The assailant was a woman, and Flowers didn't press charges.

"There's been so much concern about street incidents," Maloney explained. "I just had to act."

Again, ask yourself, "Would I help?" Are you secure enough in your individual self-worth to help others? If not, you need to be. Someone one day will need your help!

Individuality also comes as we interact with caring individuals who want the best for us. For this reason, we must accept constructive criticism and understand that discipline and love are not mutually exclusive. The opposite of love is not hate, but indifference. The worst sin toward our fellow creatures is not to hate them but to be indifferent to them (to ignore them!). That is the essence of inhumanity. To ignore or to take no interest in them, is the cruelest of all social actions. It implies there is no hope, so why bother?

If we are being disciplined for negative behavior, does it mean that the disciplinarian hates us? Quite the contrary! By taking the time to reprimand us for our unacceptable behavior, the disciplinarian is really saying, "I love you, I care. I know you can become better and I want to help you."

This philosophy is best illustrated in athletics. "When the coach stops yelling, you know he's stopped caring." One day I made it all the way through practice without his yelling at me even once. I was actually worried and thought I might lose my starting position! We need to become secure enough that when someone points out that our "house is on fire," we don't take offense but simply do what needs to be done to "extinguish the flames." We should realize he or she is merely demonstrating real love and should allow him or her to help us put out the fire of failure.

Commitment

Maintaining individuality also requires commitment—commitment to a cause with an understanding of your purpose and place in life. It's a dedication to perseverance and endurance to the end. Because everyone has the ability to change, why not accept people for who they are at present, with a vision that they can grow and become best?

This welcomes them to follow your example and accept you for who you are. In this way, we all reach our maximum potential as human beings and maintain individuality and, most important, sustain personal self-motivation.

When we understand that painters must paint, athletes must compete, businessmen must make a profit, singers must sing, and teachers must teach to be ultimately at peace with themselves, we will recognize their efforts to achieve excellence and allow them to pursue their individual goals full speed ahead! The purpose of life is for us to find out who we are and then become our very best—all we were meant to be—but then to allow others to do the same. Let us encourage and compliment one another in our individual pursuits of excellence and remember Judith Levin's words of wisdom: "Make peace with what you're not."

Make Peace with What You're Not

> While it's important to have zeniths of accomplishment, brilliance, and beauty to aim toward, it's also necessary to realize you may not quite accomplish everything you desire. And furthermore, it's perfectly OK if you don't.
> I believe that making peace with what you're not is a prerequisite to success, a milestone in growing up, and, above all, a relief. I'm relieved that I am not a philosophical scholar, or a ballet dancer, and I doubt that I'll ever write a bestseller. I do at times suffer regret, but I find it far more productive to remember my other, if shorter, list of what I am: a smart, self-aware person and a good friend. I've finally figured out that I don't have to be like everybody else. I've discovered what I really want and can realistically achieve.
> Self-acceptance doesn't rule out self-improvement. In fact, by surrendering the truly impossible dreams, I've gained the energy to tackle the possible ones.

Discovering ourselves and maintaining that individual uniqueness is one of the first and most important ingredients in the recipe of success.

In conclusion then, this entire Challenge all boils down to one thing: You can if *you* think you can. For when *you* believe it (out of your understanding of *you* as an individual) you can and will stay motivated long enough to get *your* desired end results.

"You Can if You Think You Can"

The famous football coach Vince Lombardi was once asked how he won so many championships. He replied, "I don't coach results, I coach behavior. I don't say go out and win. I say go out and do your very best. Never say never and simply play exactly like we have practiced! If everyone as individuals does their best we will win as a team. It's up to you. Bettering your individual behavior is the only way to reach peak performance. Remember, when you become satisfied and complacent as a football player, we are finished as a football team! *We* can together succeed, only if *you* think you can as an individual!"

A friend of mine, Mr. Bob Coyne from Ontario, Canada, got the idea to take a hockey team to Sweden. The idea sounded kind of unusual, but he contacted the Ontario Minor Hockey Association to find out how one could get to Scandinavia.

In his own words, he explains what happened.

> They put us onto a deal they had going with a Swedish hockey club that was looking for a host. So we agreed to host the Stockholm IFK Junior Hockey Team, which would come to Canada in December and stay until the first week of the new year. In exchange, we would go to Sweden the following year as their guests. We made preparations and the team from Sweden arrived in Canada on Boxing Day (December 26). They were the pride of Stockholm. They were fourteen- and fifteen-year-old kids, hand-picked from the Stockholm area, and were known as a notoriously tough hockey club. As their hosts, we were to provide them with a tour of seven different communities where they would play their seven exhibition games. The final game was to be against our team. When the Stockholm IFK team arrived in Canada, their hope, of course, was to win all seven

games and return home with big stories. But it was the first time away from home for these kids and after they experienced jet lag, they lost their first game by a dismal 8-to-1 score. It was a staggering defeat for them. During the second game they were a little more prepared, but again they lost 4-to-2. They lost the third and the fourth games as well. Then, in game five, they felt they were really getting back together, but again they lost, 9-to-1. At that point in the tour, which was somewhere around New Year's, we decided they needed a break in the action—a diversion to get their heads back together and maybe rebuild their confidence. We arranged a visit to Toronto with trips to see the CN Tower, the National Hockey League Hall of Fame, and other points of interest. After that we continued with the break—no hockey for two days and a light, easy outlet for the team so they could relax and recreate. We took them to where I work— the McDonald School for the Visually Impaired. The school has the biggest gymnasium in the city and its own olympic-sized swimming pool, so the idea was to have fun and loosen up in the water or on the basketball court—something totally away from competition.

We had a grand time and it came time to leave. Our bus was late in picking us up and we were sort of hanging around. So I decided that we should go to the student center and sit down and relax until the bus came. Now the student center is a very conducive place for conversation. It has indirect lighting, lots of easy chairs, and an informal environment. The chairs were set up in a circle and we sat down to wait for the bus. At that point the coach of the IFK Stockholm team asked me if there was anything I could possibly say to his team that might get them psyched up. I wasn't prepared or thinking in those terms, but I decided on the spur of the moment to see if I could touch the emotions of those kids. I started talking to them about home and about mom and dad and things like that. It got them right up off their chairs, and they were able to relate to that. Then I asked them a lot of questions that touched nerves, such as if they missed mom and dad, if the time zones and being quite a way south of Sweden were bothering them. For instance, in Stockholm they have much less daylight in winter than we do, and that was affecting them.

We talked about those kinds of things for awhile and then finally got down to hockey. We discussed what they were and were not doing and what was happening to them as a team in Canada. I reflected on the five losses in a row and how that really wasn't them at all and how they must feel about that. We exchanged ideas for awhile and I finally brought it down to the idea that what they needed was something they could reach out and relate to. I told them they needed confidence, to really believe in themselves. So I left them with a phrase that I had heard many other times and places: You Can if You Think You Can. I stared at each kid and then left the room. A few moments later the bus arrived and we left. Well, I never really thought I would convince them, but I went home prepared to reinforce the idea anyway. I made a big sign with the words You Can If You Think You Can and took it with us to the next game, held at the Six Nations Indian Reservation south of Francis. Six Nations Indians had a very monumental hockey club, and the Stockholm IFK club knew even prior to their arrival in Canada that if they lost a game it would be either to the Six Nations team or to ourselves.

Game time arrived, and the IFK team was still in the dressing room. For some reason I felt they weren't coming out, so I went to their dressing room and opened the door onto a very somber situation. Most heads were down, the coach was addressing them, but you could see they weren't up for the game. So I took the liberty of barging into the room. All heads looked up at me as I put a big smile on my face. I said, "Remember, you can if you think you can!" I waved at the coach and made my fast exit.

I then went out and hung up the sign. A minute later, the team came out on the ice and saw the sign. Spontaneously, every member jumped the boards into the players' bench, and each young man touched the sign. From there they went out onto the ice, had their warmup, and then faced off to open the game.

Very early they took a 1-to-0 lead and again they all jumped the board and touched that sign then back out for the face-off. The game continued. They scored another goal and again touched the sign. Six Nations came back to tie the game at 2, and then the Swedes went ahead 3-to-2, then 4-to-2. Six Nations tied the game in the late minutes. The game ended in a tie, but for those kids who hadn't won at all on their tour, the tie was as good as or better than a win, especially against a powerful club like Six Nations. That put them on top of the world! The noise on the bus ride home was unbelievable!

That brings us now to the last day of the tournament. Our team was their last opponent, and early the following morning, the Swedes would fly home. Game day I made arrangements to pick the coach up at his motel room for a luncheon to be held before the game to introduce the Swedish team to the press. When I went into his room he had the You Can if You Think You Can sign on the headboard of his bed. I thought it was kind of funny, but I could see that he really believed it. As we left to go to the arena he grabbed the sign and brought it with him.

When we came out of the dressing room, the first thing I noticed was the sign on the back of the Swedish players' bench. And they performed the same ritual they did before—each player touching the sign before the start of the game. This game, their final of the series, was a highly spirited contest, and they beat us by two points. And every time they scored they touched the sign. But each time they scored they also skated by my bench and shook their fists at me and grinned. There was a party for the team after the game ended, and the next morning the Swedes flew home. For the rest of the year we kept busy raising funds for our trip to Sweden, and the following December we arrived in Stockholm, for our tournament.

They have a different setup for their sports in Sweden than in Canada; they have sports clubs for nearly all sports, but they all play in the same IFK arena. The sports building is in downtown Stockholm, and we went there for a reception following our arrival. As I walked into the main lobby of this sports club, about twelve feet up on the wall hung the You Can if You Think You Can sign, nicely framed, with its story beneath it. I was surprised, happy, and choked up, all at the same time, to see it hanging there. And to this day, as far as I know, it still graces the lobby of the sports building in Stockholm, Sweden.

Does all of this positive thinking stuff really work? You bet it does! Is it truly the essence of individuality and self-motivation? You bet it is! You Can if You Think You Can!!

I, Grandfather, challenge you to accept this philosophy and live by it. May the "force" be with you always as you weather the storm, and may you stay forever young!

I read again and again and studied and contemplated motivation. It truly was the answer to everything. The success of school, friendships, relationships with family; all were based on attitude. I committed then and there to always answer the three key self-motivation questions before I started any endeavor. I committed to truthfully understanding *Why should I? What's in it for me?* and *Will it make me feel wanted and important?* before I ever began a task again. I've been asking these questions now for a week and I've accomplished more in seven days than I used to accomplish in a month. It's true! When we want to do something and develop a passionate love obsession to achieve that goal, because we want it and are working hard because we want to, we automatically break the shackles of *time* and become *task* oriented. It suddenly doesn't matter how much time it will take us to accomplish the goal, we will endure every hardship conceivable until we finish the task and turn our goals and dreams into reality.

I had studied all day long and into the late night. As I closed the sacred book to go to sleep, I couldn't help but think about all the great, fantastic things I was going to accomplish. My dreams and aspirations to win were greater than they had ever been before! But then reality hit me as I frightened myself by thinking about the long, giant task ahead of me. It was obvious that now I wanted to win more than anything else, but to have a winner there must also be a loser. Could I handle losing until I figured out how to win? I definitely wanted to be a champion but what would it take? How could I develop the winner's edge? I fell asleep and had the following dream.

A genie came to me and said, "You've lived a good life. I am sent to grant you one wish." I thought for a minute and answered, "I wish that peace and love and liberty will fill the whole earth." The genie replied, "That's a noble wish, but we don't deal in fruits here, we deal only in seeds."

I interpreted that to mean that I shouldn't get solutions mixed up with symptoms; that I should cut through the fruits of the world conflict and focus in on the seeds that are causing it. I then realized this philosophy also applied to drug and alcohol abuse. We're spending most of our time and money dealing with the fruits (the symptoms of the users) when we should be spending time and money on the seeds (low self-esteem, loser friends and poor family life) that are causing the abuse.

In this mind-set I asked the genie to grant the wish of answering the secret to being a winner. I asked him how to be a champion. He simply answered, "Winning does not require elaborate, giant steps and methods. It only requires constant commitment to little steps. The difference between good and great is just a little bit of extra effort. Some say it's raw talent; some say it's coaching; and some say it's desire. I say these are all part of the solution, but the real seed is simply hard work on a daily basis—the little bit makes the big difference!"

Then the genie surprised me when he motioned and invited, "Come with me through a time line of champions and see for yourself. The 'force' is with you which allows a special experience. Let me help you relive some of the past. I will show you the seeds of the winner's edge."

The genie took me by the hand, somehow materialized me, floating me through the wall of my bedroom, and together we sped quickly into the past in a hurried, blurry vision to a locker room at the University of South Carolina. There we began our journey through time and the genie told me it was my responsibility to keep record of what we saw and the interpretation of what winning was as I perceived it. I awakened the next morning from the dream and immediately wrote it down. Challenge 7 is my personal account of my dream experiences. I have verified all of them as real history. The stories are true!

CHALLENGE 7

The Winner's Edge: Steps to Peak Performance

Dick Vermeil said, "If you don't invest very much, then defeat doesn't hurt very much and winning isn't very exciting."

In South Carolina I saw a sign on the locker room wall that said: The Difference between Good and Great Is a Little Bit of Extra Effort. I pondered its meaning until I found the answer in another experience. We flew back in time to 1984.

It was the year of the exciting summer Olympic Games. We were now in Colorado Springs, Colorado, guests at the Olympic training facility. During the visit we went to watch the U.S. boxing team work out. I talked to the coach for about thirty minutes, watched the heavyweights blast each other, and then turned to leave. Just before I walked out of the gym, I looked back one more time and saw an inspiring scene. Standing on the floor outside the ring was a young boxer dripping with sweat, bent over, out of breath, with his hands grasping a jump rope. He paused for a moment and looked up at a sign painted in big bold letters on the wall: A Champion Fights One More Round. Not more than ten seconds passed until he stood back up, tall, straight, proud, and determined, and started strenuously jumping rope again. He showed that the difference between ordinary and extraordinary is that little "extra." He proved the truth of Woody Hayes's words: "Paralyze resistance with persistence." He demonstrated that the only difference between a big shot and a little shot is the little shot who kept shooting. We are what we repeatedly do. Winning, then, is Excellence, and Excellence is not an act but a habit.

As we continued our flash through the past, I realized some of us aren't thrilled by sports, but what makes a champion is always the same regardless of our field or interest. Mario Andretti said, "Desire is the key to motivation, but it's the determination and commitment to an unrelenting pursuit of your goal—a commitment to excellence—that will enable you to attain the success you seek. What makes a champion oftentimes is determined only by a fraction of time and effort."

Extra Effort Makes Perseverance Pay

The genie now took me back in time to the Summer Olympic Games in Melbourne, Australia. Here I learned that the difference between good and great can be hardly measured. It was the half-mile race. Out of the eight men in the race, five of them had held the world record at one time or another. How would you like to come up to the starting line knowing that a tenth of a second would be the difference between first and fifth place? How would you deal with the stress and nervousness of knowing the smallest mistake would cost you any kind of respectable finish?

The runners took their marks. Pow! The starting gun went off, and down the track, around the curve, came the sprinters—all running for victory. Arnie Sole, an American, took the lead. Right behind Arnie were four world record holders, breathing down his neck. He set a terrific pace even against the stiff wind on the back stretch, and at the end of the first lap he had a startling lead. The bell sounded for the last lap. Halfway around the track Arnie started to fatigue. The pace was just too much for him to continue, and Tom Courtney started to make his move. With less than 100 yards to go, a gust of wind hit all of them in the face and almost stopped them in their tracks. Right then Sole ran completely out of gas. Courtney's lungs were burning, his legs went numb, he had to quit. But as Johnson passed him by with only ten yards left, Courtney, running almost unconscious, fought his way back to lunge at the tape and win by eight inches. He collapsed at the finish line and had to be revived five times. He couldn't even walk. They had to postpone the victory ceremony for over an hour until he had the strength to attend. This is what is meant when we hear the phrase *You've got to have desire!* This is the difference between good and great! This is the *winner's edge!*

We then flew ahead to the 1974 Kentucky Derby. The winning jockey was paid $2,700. Less than two seconds later, the jockey who crossed the finish line in fourth place was paid $30.

We then flew back in time to 1982, Gordon Johncock won the Indianapolis 500 motor car race by only sixteen hundredths of a second—the length of his car. Yet, his payoff was well over ten times that of the second-place finisher.

The genie and I then paused and stopped in to watch a baseball game. What a great lesson we learned there!

Miles of Difference Between .300 and .200

We can all relate to the world of baseball. When a player has a batting average of .300 it simply means he had a base hit in three out of every ten times at bat. Sounds easy, right? For this three-out-of-ten effort, the few fortunate superstars who can maintain this average, year in and year out, are paid maximum salaries. They endorse underwear, speak at celebrity dinners, and appear on charity telethons. They are nationally recognized heroes with posters and trading cards.

Now contrast these .300 hitters with .200 hitters. Who are some of the past .200 hitter superstars? There aren't any! They come a dime a dozen and aren't around in the league long enough to ever become stars. A manager can always find a .200 hitter. They are traded as often as a manager changes his dirty socks!

What is the difference between a .300 hitter and a .200 hitter? Only one hit in every ten times at bat. And if the batters let the count go to full count three balls, two strikes, the difference between a .300 hitter and a .200 hitter is only one hit in every sixty pitches!

How does this relate to you and me? The difference between good and great is one more effective minute worked in every sixty on your homework, one more productive day in every sixty! It's one more effort to mend a faltering relationship in every sixty attempts and one more effective sports or music practice in every sixty.

McMahon's "Never Quit" Pass

Jim McMahon, the great quarterback for the Super Bowl champion Chicago Bears, is the epitome of extra effort and proves to all of us the validity of this statement.

The genie and I traveled again back in time to 1980. It was December 19, 1980, Holiday Bowl III. Jim McMahon's nationally ranked BYU Cougars were playing against Southern Methodist University. There were four minutes and seven seconds left to play in the game. SMU was winning, 45 to 25. BYU called time out and coach Lavell Edwards motioned McMahon to the sideline. Edwards said, "Let's go for a big one and see if we can score one more time and restore respectability before the game ends."

McMahon got upset. "Coach, what do you mean? We're not quitting! It's not over until it's over!" McMahon went back onto the field, called the team together, and said, "We're gonna win!" The very next play he threw a bomb—touchdown! BYU recovered the ensuing onsides kick and scored on a one yard scamper by a running back. BYU kicked off, held SMU for three downs, and then blocked the punt and recovered the ball with thirteen seconds left on the clock. McMahon's first two passes were incomplete, but on the very next play, with three seconds left on the clock, McMahon completed a forty-six-yard bomb to Clay Brown in the end zone. Brown leaped high in the air to catch it and the game was tied! Gunther came onto the field and kicked the extra point. BYU won, 46 to 45.

McMahon was runner-up to Marcus Allen for the Heisman Trophy, was a first-round pick by the Chicago Bears, and was named Rookie of the Year in the National Football League.

In 1984, Doug Flutie proved the same thing and with his Boston College teammates won an important game in exactly the same miracle catch—a come-from-behind maneuver. Flutie also won the Heisman! These two athletes not only have superior talent, they have superior determination and drive to do a little "something more."

The difference between good and great, between winning and losing, truly and simply is extra effort. Sure, it's important to have good practice facilities and great coaching, and some talent to go with it. But without extraordinary determination, extra desire and dedication to excel, becoming a champion remains only a dream.

I realize we hear the words *dedication* and *desire* quite often, but let's take the time to examine them. Do we have to work out twice as hard or twice as long as our opponents do to demonstrate dedication and become champions? No! Just a little bit of extra time and effort makes the big difference!

Peter Vidmar, a good friend and gold medal Olympic

gymnast, proved this true in his Olympic experience. To achieve championship performance, Pete didn't work out twice as long as the other gymnasts; he worked out only fifteen minutes longer each day. That doesn't seem to be any great extra sacrifice, right? But when you add up fifteen minutes a day for a year, you find that Peter Vidmar worked out ninety-one hours and fifteen minutes longer than the other gymnasts on his championship team.

Passive Power Can Prevail

We gain a slight edge on winning not just through extra "active effort" but through extra "passive effort" as well.

For instance, if you're playing football and you're on defense, look at the offensive lineman's fingertips when he crouches in his stance. If his fingernails are white it means he is leaning forward and applying heavy pressure on his hand. That means a running play is coming because the only thing a big guy can do when his weight is forward is to fire out and block. If there is no pressure on his fingertips, he is probably planning to stand up, pass block, or pull to the side. In this case, give yourself the winner's edge and take advantage of the situation by perhaps widening your alignment to give yourself a better pass rush or a better angle to take on a trap block or head off a wide running play.

We can also use this passive extra effort as we observe the behavior of others. Subtle actions give us an idea of the type of person we are dealing with long before we do business. For example, when you are eating, glance at your associate's dining habits. If he or she seasons the food before tasting it, it implies that they jump to conclusions—he or she is not willing to gather all the information before making a decision. Such an observation and conclusion may change the way you approach your business dealings with that person.

When you play golf, don't think about the absurdity of

hitting a little white ball as far as you can and chasing it. Rather, look for the messages being sent by those you are golfing with.

Billy Casper told me that we can learn more about a person on a golf course than anywhere else. It's because golf brings out many emotions and puts them on parade for all to see. When you realize the subtle implications of certain actions of your partners, it's amazing how successfully you'll be able to deal with them off the course.

Mark McCormack, business manager of some of the world's great athletes, explains his observations. "A 'gimme' (give me putt) is a short putt, usually two feet or less, conceded to the golfer by his opponent. This means he or she doesn't have to hit the ball and instead picks it up and moves on to the next hole. Some people refuse all gimmes, insisting on hitting every shot and accurately recording the results. Others don't wait for the okay; they just assume it's a gimme. These are usually the big egos who almost believe they can command the ball into the hole. Business translation: They won't ask you for a favor either—they expect it!"

Before we go on, I must reiterate that we can get our desired results from our associates in most situations if we just use our imagination to give us the slight edge. For instance, the day I checked into the university, my football coach assigned me my dorm roommate. He laughed and said he was a big, tall lineman who snored a lot and that I would never get any sleep. On my way to my room I decided to get the upper hand. The moment I met my roommate, I grabbed him and gave him a big kiss right on the lips! That night and most other nights he just lay there with at least one eye on me at all times. He couldn't snore if he didn't dare to sleep and the problem was solved. I always slept like a baby!

The genie then whisked me away to look at someone who has a lifelong commitment to excellence through extra effort.

A Champ in the Cotton Fields and on the Baseball Diamond

George Foster, the great professional baseball superstar, makes $2 million a year. That's approximately $5,479 each day, 365 days each year. The New York Mets who were the last team to pay his salary contend he was well worth it. What makes George Foster so special? Not one thing, but many little things all mixed together. Sure, George had been able to maintain a .300 batting average for most of his long career. Sure, he was a national hero and helped sell tickets to the ball games. Sure, he was a home run king who electrified the crowd with his game-winning hits. Sure, he's handsome; polite; and a good, clean, all-American role model. But there's even more to this extra-effort player. His winning wasn't a sometime thing—it was an all-the-time thing!

George Foster was born in 1948 in the segregated town of Tuscaloosa, Alabama. One day when he was six years old he was sitting on the steps in front of his home watching his big brother and sister play catch with a ball. He knew he could play, too, if just given the chance, but they said George was too small and would get hurt if he tried.

He soon got bored, grabbed another small rubber ball, and walked out into the cotton fields near his home. The cotton plants with their many fluffy, white puffs always looked pretty from a distance, but when George got in the middle of the field, he shuddered, because like most black children growing up in the south, he had to pick cotton just like the older folks.

George didn't mind working hard, and when the boss gave him a large sack to fill with cotton, he picked for hours, bent over in the hot sun. He would rather have played catch, but he knew he had a job to do.

One day the whistle finally blew, ending the eight-hour work day. George hated the job, but he had picked so much cotton he was sure he would be paid well. He dragged his overstuffed bag to the weigh station and watched as the scales tipped eighty-seven pounds, more than twice George's body weight! George smiled a proud smile and politely held out his hand to be paid. The boss handed him eighty-seven cents—a penny a pound for eight hours of work!

George said thank you, turned, and began to walk home. But his bottled-up frustration at poor pay and no control to change it was finally too much to hold inside. He took out his little rubber ball and started throwing it as hard and as high into the air as he could, trying to hit the sky. George recalls, "I never did hit the sky, but I made a commitment right then that one day I'd be strong enough to hit a star."

Why is George Foster's story so important? Because George has never changed his desire to hit the stars and do a little bit more! From picking more cotton than anyone else to taking more baseballs in batting practice than anyone else!

George moved with his mother to Hawthorne, California, when he was young, and finally got to play organized baseball when he was twelve years old. He struck out his first time at bat, but on his second try, George smashed the first pitch over the fence for a home run. This indicated what was to come. He loved baseball, made all-star teams, worked out with weights to strengthen his frail body, and eventually graduated with honors (his batting average in the classroom was also high) from mostly white Leuzinger High School in 1966. From there, George went to El Camino Junior College, hoping to be discovered and one day play professional baseball.

Willie Mays was George's idol, and George's dream was to join Willie on the San Francisco Giants team. At junior college, a pro scout saw George play, and he was drafted by the Giants in 1968, eventually realizing his boyhood dream—to play side by side with his idol, Willie Mays. George was later traded to the Cincinnati Reds, where he went into a drastic slump and was demoted to the minors.

Though discouraged, George hung tough through a few years of hard times and self-doubt, and the rest is baseball history.

Here is the key: each day Foster did a little bit more than anyone else on his team. He ran more sprints, caught more fly balls, hit more pitches—that's how badly he wanted to succeed. Even though he was depressed he always managed to pull himself up and continue doing "just a little more."

In 1977, after having been called back to the big league Reds, George won the National League Most Valuable Player Award. He led the league three years in a row in runs batted in and is only the fourth player in National League History to have hit more than fifty home runs in a season. He has also led the league in home runs, total bases, and most runs scored. George Foster is a living legend who truly exemplifies the statement: "The difference between good and great is a little bit of extra effort!"

Perfect Practice Makes Perfect

George Foster's story exemplifies a second philosophical statement that goes hand in hand with extra effort—consistency. George became one of the best in baseball through practice, practice, practice. And not just practicing anything, but practicing the right thing. To succeed, we must know how and what and when to practice. We can no longer believe the popular statement, "Practice makes perfect." It's not true! "Perfect Practice makes perfect" is the advice we really need to follow!

Perfect practice comes as we figure out *what* to practice. Knowing *what* to practice is the key to consistency.

For instance, if you have trouble with fractions on your math tests, don't just study the problems that come easily to you. Learn how to do the hard fraction problems and then practice doing them! If you've been playing in a golf tournament and have successfully hit the ball well with all of your clubs except for your putter, do you go to the driving range and practice with your driver? Then, use the time-tested, best teacher: spaced repetition. Not improperly but properly. You correct and fix what is broken! Then, you repeat it over and over until it becomes a new habit. Any other way only reinforces your errors. That's why many people who play golf their entire lives never see their game improving. They get off one good shot, then screw up the next; or they'll play well for eight holes and suddenly get a triple bogey on the ninth. Their game is inconsistent because they failed to learn to swing properly in the first place, and all their practice reinforces their bad habits and perpetuates their failure. Somewhere there is a flaw in their stance, grip, or swing, and the longer they play incorrectly, the more difficult it is to correct their bad habits, even with the best instructor. Eventually, the inherent flaw in their game catches up to them and continually plagues them forever!

This holds true in life! Therefore, as you continue to perfect your strengths, don't forget to practice especially hard on your current weaknesses. When another weakness arises, just repeat the practice procedure again and again and again until that broken part is also fixed. Each time you work or play, take time to evaluate and pinpoint your weaknesses and then work to perfect them. Knowing what and when to practice is the key to consistency and the key ingredient in the recipe for becoming a winner.

The genie then whisked me way back in time to see one of my heroes. Ted Williams was one of the greatest hitters in all of professional baseball history. But he wasn't always a great hitter; he had to perfectly practice his way to the top. In the first several years that he played in the major leagues, Williams used to pull the ball to right field. In fact, he pulled it to right field so often that the opposing teams automatically shifted their defenders to the right, leaving a giant hole on the left side of the field. As time went on, Williams realized he was hitting more and more balls right at the outfielders. His inability to hit the ball to the left was costing him several hits and many batting average percentage points.

In one of the first games of the following season, Ted came up to bat against the Cleveland Indians, who, like every other team, shifted dramatically toward right field when he was up. On the first pitch, Williams surprised everyone by hitting an extra base hit into left field. The next time at bat, Cleveland stayed in the famous "Ted Williams shift," overplaying him to the right, and again Williams slammed an extra base hit into the hole in left field.

Everyone was puzzled except Ted. He had spent the entire off-season and a lot of the spring-training period just practicing hitting the ball to the left. Obviously, his extra effort and perfect practice paid off. Opposing teams stopped shifting when Ted came up to bat, and he became one of the greatest all-time hitters in the game. Through perfect practice he turned his weakness into a strength and became a superior player. In 1941, Ted Williams had a .406 batting average, which has never been matched or beaten.

In 1980, George Brett came close to beating Williams with a .390 average. And how did he do it? Brett not only perfectly practiced, but he took it one step further. Before he ever walked out onto the field, George "visualized" himself hitting the ball. He would concentrate so hard that he could actually see the ball coming from the pitcher's hand. He could see the bat hitting the ball and hear the crowd roar—he could picture himself winning the game.

Visualization: The Key to Consistency

This visualization technique works! All the greats in all fields of interest have exercised visualization. Long before they won, they saw themselves winning; they felt the emotions of thrilling victory.

Visualization is both the first step and the last step in reaching consistency. Visualization starts our motivation motor running and then helps us to maintain it during our extra-effort process.

Visualization not only gives us the foresight and direction necessary for us to practice, it also allows us to practice a specific circumstance.

For instance, let's say our basketball team is behind by one point. Ten seconds remain on the clock, and I have to dribble the length of the basketball court and score the game-winning basket. If I practice dribbling and shooting enough times so that I no longer fear that pressure situation, if and when the situation really happens, I will be prepared to do what I've visualized and practiced so many times before.

Could this make-believe situation ever occur? My friend Danny Ainge, formerly of the Boston Celtics and now of the Sacramento Kings, had a classic answer.

When Danny made one of the most incredible game-winning plays in the history of college basketball, he knew ahead of time he would succeed. There were ten seconds left on the clock in an NCAA playoff game, and Danny's Brigham Young team was one point behind Notre Dame. The ball was passed into Ainge and the clock started to tick off those final seconds. He dazzlingly dribbled around two guys to midcourt, dribbled behind his back while avoiding another player, changed hands dribbling past a fourth opponent, and, at the buzzer, leaped high over the last Notre Dame player to lay the ball into the basket and single-handedly score the game-winning points.

Even before Danny had passed half court, his brother in the stands had already started to clap and cheer as if Danny had already made the basket. After the game, Danny's brother was interviewed about his premature ecstasy over winning the game. His reply: "I had seen Danny make those same moves so many times in practice that I knew for sure he could easily make them again. And he did!"

Danny added later, "It's funny. When I practice, I make up pressure situations in my mind. A teammate would count down the last ten seconds and I would dash down the court, put on a few razzle dazzle moves, shoot the high-flying layup, and win the imaginary game. I must have won a thousand games in my mind before I won this real game today. There was no pressure on me today because I had visualized what I would do so many times in my dreams."

Danny Ainge proves true the thought that pressure is not something that is naturally there. It's created only when you question your own ability. And when you know what you can do, there's never any question about succeeding.

I challenge you to start giving every situation everything you've got when less would be sufficient. Start Visualizing yourself winning and then perfectly practice, practice, and practice. Remember that perfect prior practice prevents poor performance. And then, don't take my word for it. Go ahead and prove to yourself that the difference between good and great is a little bit of extra effort! The following poem is by a friend of mine who truly understands the principles discussed in this challenge. It is a fitting climax conclusion and reminder of what it takes to capture the "Winner's Edge" and be a champion.

Do You Want to Be a Champion?
by William T. Braithwaite

Do you want to run till your lungs burn tight?
Do you want to hustle with all your might?
Do you want your shirt soaking with sweat?

Work, my son, you'll be a Champion yet.
Can you take bad breaks in a hard-fought game?
Can you be way down and fight just the same?
Can you face the task with a jaw that's set?

Steady, my son, you'll be a Champion yet.
Is your spirit inside a burning flame?
Is your "want to" strong and feeble and lame?
Is your eye on target, a goal to be met?

Fire up, young man, you'll be a Champion yet.
Do you feel the sting of the blisters you've worn?
Do your legs grow limp from "bucking" the storm?
Do your eyes turn red from salt and sweat?

Courage, my son, you'll be a Champion yet.
Can you sit on the bench and back your team?
Can you cheer for others but keep your dream?
Can you play your role, not stew and fret?
Can you lift up your game going down to the wire?

Can you rise from defeat once the verdict is set?
Desire, my son, you'll be a Champion yet.
It's not in the score as much in the mind.
It's not in the glory, the fame, or their kind.
It lies in the maxim, "You must give to get."
Hang in there, son, you'll be a Champion yet!

I, Daniel, by the power of the high Kahuna in me by
Grandfather, leave you with his usual exhortation: I challenge you to accept this philosophy and live by it! May
the "force" be with you always as you weather the storm,
and may you stay forever young! End of challenge 7.

CHALLENGE 8

Equality, Action, and Endurance Equal Control

Francis Quarles wrote, "I see no virtue where I smell no sweat."

To help us understand this concept of hard work and endurance to the end, and why we should accept obstacles as opportunities to show what we are made of, I wish to explain some things.

To begin this challenge, we must first understand the importance of taking responsibility for who we are and what we do.

Dr. Stephen E. Cosgrove has researched data-based human tendencies that he calls "four myths."

There are four myths of responsibility for one's feelings.

1. I can make you feel good.
2. I can make you feel bad.
3. You can make me feel good.
4. You can make me feel bad.

The very bottom line is that no one can make us feel any way than the way we choose to feel. The individual is in charge! The option is only to relinquish or not to relinquish the power to feel to someone else. But there are many who don't understand the constant option to take control of their feelings, actions, and lives. They believe they have no choice and always blame others (family, neighborhood, economy, friends) for their lack of success.

If it is my personality to let others control my feelings, I am weak. When someone says "you jerk," they are not forcing me to feel bad. They are inviting me to feel bad, but I am still in control! No one can make you feel inferior without your own consent. Dr. Cosgrove further continues, "The only thing you are not in charge of is whether or not you are in charge—because you are always in charge!"

In addition to the four myths of responsibility for feelings, there are four cop-outs for not taking charge. Here are Cosgrove's explanations:

1. The Gene Theory. "It's all in your chromosomes—it's hereditary. You can't do anything about your constitutional genetic makeup. You're stuck with the way you were born because the generations before you were in the same boat. Your personality is negative and ornery because your mother's personality is negative."

2. The Cosmic Theory. "The world is the way it is, and you can't do anything about it, and it's not going to change, so give it up and don't bother me!"

3. The Astrology Theory. "You were born under a specific sign of the zodiac, on a certain date, and therefore, your life has been predetermined. You must have a certain personality, and this will happen to you this month because you are a Pisces fish or a Taurus bull. The stars control your life."

4. The Devil-Made-Me-Do-It Theory. "I was overcome and had no control." Wrong! You started out in total control of the situation and chose to lose control. You allowed yourself to let your emotions overload on the temptation and the situation got out of hand. Our conscience never fails us—only our desire to follow it decreases as we continue to do what we know we should not do.

This is not new doctrine! Religious holy books point this out when they claim, "God will not suffer you to be tempted above that you are able; but will with the temptation also make a way to escape, that you may be able to bear it." So, if we do fall and give in to a negative situation that results in negative personal behavior, who is at fault? Are we not always in control and, therefore, always responsible for our feelings and actions?

Can you see the mistakes we are making as we subscribe to one or more of these false assumptions and popular perspectives? Can you sense the self-inflicted barriers we are placing on our minds, imaginations, goal-setting processes, and expectations as we use these cop-outs and look for excuses for failure instead of reasons for success? If so, let us commit to the challenge of change. We can no longer just talk the talk; we need to walk the walk! Life isn't a spectator sport! We must get involved and take responsibility for our success process. We must seek the answers to where we began, what it's all about, what's holding us back, why we are the way we are at present, and how to change for the best. Let's reflect on our beginnings.

Babies babble the same in any country in the world. But as they grow to adulthood, their thinking, speaking, and actions begin to reflect characteristics of their environments. Many bizarre discoveries have been made that verify this fundamental truth.

There is documentation that as many as seventeen children have lived and been raised by wild animals. When discovered, the children were much like their animal guardians in actions and characteristics. Here are two of the stories that illustrate all of the seventeen examples.

In 1344, hunters in the German kingdom of Hesse captured a boy, approximately twelve years of age, who had been living in the wild. Wolves had brought him food and dug holes to shelter him at night. The boy ran on all fours and had an extraordinary ability to leap long distances.

In October 1920, the Rev. J. A. L. Singh captured two girls, one about three years old and the other around five, who had lived with a pack of wolves near the village of Midnapore, India. Named Amala and Kamala by Singh, the girls were mute except for occasional growling sounds, walked on all fours, and loved to eat raw meat. After a year in civilization, Amala died. Kamala eventually acquired a forty-five word vocabulary before her death in 1929.

When you look around it's obvious that we are products of our up-bringing and environment. If an adult is undesirable and disagreeable, it is because he or she was brought up wrong.

Abilities can be nurtured or suppressed in any child. On one hand, children grow and cultivate talents and abilities through positive reinforcement. But on the other hand, negative input retards and distorts the human development process. For this reason, even a Mozart had the possibility of becoming tone deaf, depending upon the way he was raised.

Shinichi Suzuki, a world-renowned psychologist, has proven through years of testing and study that the subconscious mind knows neither right nor wrong. It only captures the input and stores it. Suzuki took this data and discovered that people who can't carry a tune heard off-pitch, sour lullabies growing up. They were only exposed to negative incorrect input. To stop the tone deafness, Suzuki simply reversed the negative input process and replaced it with positive correct melodies. At which time the number of correct notes (the mind had newly registered) outnumbered the sour notes (that had previously been "reality"), the child or adult snapped out of it and from then on could carry a tune.

It's true! We are not born, we are made! Suzuki writes, "If Einstein, Goethe, and Beethoven had been born during the Stone Age, wouldn't they likewise have had only the cultural ability and education of men of the Stone Age? The converse is also true: If I were to receive a babe of the Stone Age and educate him or her, before long, he or she would be able to play a violin sonata by Beethoven as well as any young person of today."

Looking at our potential in another way, adults are simply mature babies. Regardless of our age, we still possess the ability to change and grow to be the best we can be. If we find that we are not progressing, the solution is simple. We must go back to the basics. We must rethink our incorrect perceptions and alter our negative environments and then repeat the new positive input enough times until we replace the old. It really is this simple. What goes in, sticks, and definitely comes out. We can change our actions and the persons we are by simply changing what goes into our minds. Learning tools and techniques aren't enough. We must remember "ACPP."

We must change our *A*ttitude, develop a strong *C*ommitment to change, improve our *P*erformance or behavior by learning the necessary new skills, and follow through on our commitment through *P*articipation. Therefore, the way we improve quality is to participate in the changing, self-improvement process. "Tell me and I forget. Show me and I remember. But involve me and I learn."

This challenge, then, is obviously about personal involvement in learning why we should look at obstacles as growth opportunities, why we can and should use them as stepping stones instead of stumbling blocks, and why we can change, adapt, and become better. Sure, we are products of our environment, but we can change, if necessary, and become all that we were meant to be.

Because change is sometimes difficult, the following three philosophies should be understood. When we accept them, positive change and an acceptance of obstacles will rapidly occur.

1776 and Now: Equality Is the Same

"We hold these Truths to be self-evident, that all Men are created equal, that they are endowed by their Creator with certain unalienable Rights, that among these are Life, Liberty, and the Pursuit of Happiness."

This now-immortal statement subscribed to by our fore-fathers poses some questions: What is the meaning of equality as it pertains to people? Does it mean that all mankind must be alike? Does it mean that all mankind should be elevated up or pushed down to a common place? Does it mean that all mankind, regardless of individual talents and abilities, will always have to remain the same?

Of course not! This equality spoken of in the 1700s reveals that equality means the right to become unequal; the right to voice our views; the right to worship; the right to work. Remember that some men dream of worthy accomplishments, while others stay awake and do them. We need to oppose the kind of equality that restricts the willing man or woman to the pace of the unwilling. Equality means opportunity for each person to rise to the levels that each of our personal energies, abilities, and desires will take us to.

When we understand equality we will dismiss the often-heard liberal psychology that we should take more from the rich and give to the poor. This thought is absurd and does not enhance equality. There are a lot of "poor" people who should be cared for, but there are also "poor" people who don't have to be poor. They can work but won't; they have no self-pride and are content to take a dole because they are lazy or because they can't find a job in their field.

It doesn't matter who we are or where we live, if we want to badly enough and are willing to work, we can find someone who will pay us to help them. Especially if we take pride and take time to qualify ourselves to do something! Equality doesn't mean security. It means we want equal opportunity to work and prosper according to our desires—equal opportunity to become unequal.

The second philosophy we must understand in order to effectively deal with obstacles is that we are never entirely on our own.

I once heard a conversation where a father and his son were discussing a risky situation. The father, as fathers usually are, was cautious. The son, as sons usually are, was excited, somewhat reckless, and eager. The son said, "Don't worry. If I do it, I'll take full responsibility. I'll be completely on my own."

I know we think this sounds reassuring, but it is not. What the son failed to see was that no one is ever entirely on his own. There is always a responsibility for himself and for others.

Richard Evans explains, "A pilot who takes out an airplane under unsafe circumstances may assure the ground crew that he will take full responsibility for his actions. But it simply isn't so. When someone is overdue, missing, in danger or distress, others begin to worry and search. When an accident occurs, rescue crews, families, friends, and sometimes whole communities immediately go to work, not counting the cost and at much risk to themselves."

There is no way of endangering ourselves, or doing what we should not do without its having an effect on others. And a person can never say it's only his or her own life, or his or her own health, or his or her own reputation, or own name, or own future, or own failure. Seldom, if ever, does anyone ever risk anything altogether alone. Seldom, if ever, is any act confined in its effect to the one person who perpetrates it.

Mr. Evans is absolutely right! And we must understand this philosophy and be able to live it in order to deal with obstacles and succeed. Our personal success or failure does affect everyone! An understanding of this prepares us for the third philosophical success attitude: "Make the most of yourself—for that is all there is of you."

Be All That You Can Be

A highly recognized television commercial gets us excited to "Be all that you can be." I feel this is the greatest motto ever coined. It says it all! It says you're important, take time for yourself, make yourself happy, and go for it! It means that no matter what happens, positive or negative, you will respond the best you can and make the most of every second, every hour, and every day of your life. You will take all that you have and do what you have to do to accomplish your goals. Lubbock said, "When we have done our best, we should wait the result in peace." It definitely is a great deal better to do all the things you should do than to spend the rest of your life wishing you had!

Two stories illustrate this point.

The first time James ever felt successful and important was in junior high school. But one week he got beat up by a bully every day after school. On Sunday night he felt so dejected and depressed that he wanted to commit suicide. He changed his mind because he thought everyone would think he had done something wrong and decided to postpone the suicide until another time. The next day, Monday, on the bus ride home from school, five guys offered to beat up the bully for James. Then his mother offered to pick him up from school each night to avoid the hassle. These offers were fine, but they didn't change the situation or help solve the problem. It wasn't until James decided to face his obstacle head on and do something to stick up for himself that things changed.

James turned down the offers for assistance and said, "No thanks. If I dodge what's causing my fear and walk away from my problems today, I'll have to run for a lifetime." You ask, "And what if he loses?" At least he loses a righteous fight with his self-pride intact. And a loss really isn't a loss if he doesn't have to carry that fear around inside of him anymore! We all need to ponder, "Am I fit company for the person I want to become? If not now, when?" And we must be if we are ever to be at peace with ourselves and be all we can be.

Finish What You Start

Bo Boberg wanted to be a professional baseball player. He knew that in order to make the big leagues he would have to be special, so he developed a pitch all his own—the "nothing ball." It worked only if you threw it straight overhand and followed through low. This forced him to come down hard on his left leg. Bo perfected this self-invented pitch and became a star. At the age of seventeen, he signed his first pro baseball contract.

During his first year in the pros, Bo was riding his motorcycle when a truck hit him broadside. His left leg—the leg he needed to effectively pitch with—was severed. The accident quickly ended his career.

Years later, Bo was asked to play in an old-timer's baseball game. He was the starting pitcher and struck the first three batters out. But this isn't what really revealed his character. When it was Bo's turn to bat, a teammate asked if he needed someone to run for him. Bo abruptly answered, "No way!" promptly hit a ground ball to the third baseman, and hobbled all the way to first base. Even though he was out by fifteen feet, Bo still ran all the way. The second Bo touched first base, the whole grandstand stood up and cheered this amazing display of pure guts, determination, and truly being all that he could be. Let us remember that anything worth doing is worth doing right. Anything worth starting is worth finishing.

Let us now shift gears and explore even a higher philosophic truism that will capsulize and mobilize our ability to deal with obstacles!

Ronald Osborn said, "Unless you try to do something

beyond what you have already mastered, you will never grow."

Babe Ruth said, "I always try to follow through. Stopping at third base adds no more to the score than striking out."

In contrast, the mama whale said to the baby whale, "Remember, it's only when you get to the top and start blowing off that people throw harpoons at you." Successful living is found somewhere within the framework of these three statements. So why do we make it so hard on ourselves?

For instance, most individuals talk big, but very few act big. This is one of life's biggest problems, for you can't build a reputation on what you intended to do. It's been said that "what you do speaks so loudly that I cannot hear what you say." Doing nothing is the most tiring thing in the world because you can never take time out to rest!

How many individuals do you know who fit into this mold and even seem to say to the fire, "You give me warmth and I'll give you some wood." They have it backwards! And then wait until all the conditions are perfectly right before starting.

What does all this mean? Simply put, it's not what you have that counts, but what you do with what you have that matters. "It's not the size of the dog in the fight, but the size of the fight in the dog." "Put your money where your mouth is." Is this a new revelation? Of course not! We all know this, and that is the point. There is a big difference between knowing and doing.

For example, we all know from our educational experience that if we study harder and smarter we get better scores on our exams. But how many of us do it? We all know that if we work out longer and harder in the gym we will get stronger. But how many of us do it?

Doing is the key! Doing is what makes life simple. Doing builds strength of character. Consequently, if you're made of the right stuff, a hard fall results only in a high bounce.

You'll quickly turn your excuses for failure into reasons for success. And as you rise higher each time you fall you will soon notice that those who complain about the way the ball bounces are usually the ones who dropped it! They are the ones who talk big and don't act big. They are the ones who think the world owes them a living and who are blaming the world for their failure.

Remember Benjamin Disraeli's words: "The secret of success in life is for a man to be ready for his opportunity when it comes." Too many of us are in the planning stage and never get into the *go* stage. Act, don't react; don't talk, do! Benjamin Franklin reminds us, "Dost thou love life? Then do not squander time; for that is the stuff life is made of."

In theory, all this sounds great. But what about realistic application? How do we deal with stress and pressure and obstacles in everyday life and still keep going?

Are you depressed? Insecure? Tense? Experts now believe that acting the way you wish you felt—happy, confident, relaxed—can actually help you feel that way.

One day my friend was deeply discouraged and depressed. He usually dealt with the blues by avoiding people until the bad mood passed. But on this day he had an appointment with an important business associate, so he put on a false face. He faced the "stress" head on! Throughout the meeting he laughed; joked; acted happy, confident, and secure; and was the good-natured person of old. What was the result?

Within minutes he was no longer stressed out and depressed. And it wasn't just temporary. His bad mood left for as long as he wanted it to leave. He had stumbled onto an important psychological principle: "Acting as If" will help us feel the way we want to feel. "Acting as if" we're happy ensures that we become happy. A positive or negative attitude is our individual choice.

EIGHT QUICK SUGGESTIONS TO "DO" WHEN DEALING WITH STRESS

1. If you're down in the dumps, smile to cheer yourself up. Even laugh—think of something pleasant or funny and enjoy it. Listen to a comedian; watch a humorous movie.
2. Relax. This reduces anxiety and fear. To relax, first lie down in a comfortable position. Now flex the muscles in your hands and feet as tensely as you can. Hold your fists for five counts, then gently let go. Breathe in while you do it, exhale on completion. Close your eyes and feel the tension leave your body.
3. Look your best. When you take the extra time to primp and dress for success, you increase your self-confidence. If you're overweight, don't feel sorry for yourself. Fix what is broken and start today to lose weight!
4. Talk out your challenges or write your feelings down and talk to yourself on paper (wad up the paper and throw it away when you're through). Problems can get blown out of proportion when they're bottled up inside. Let the stressful pressure out!
5. Breathe. Next time you're stressed out, check your breathing. You'll probably find you're taking short, shallow breaths and using only your chest to breathe. Taking a deep, relaxing breath and making an effort to breathe deeply and slowly is one of the quickest ways to reverse your feelings of stress.
6. Cry. There is evidence that tears may help the body rid itself of potentially harmful chemicals produced in times of stress. Studies show that people with intestinal problems are more likely to regard crying as a sign of weakness or loss of control than healthy people.
7. Have fun. Go to the beach, go bowling, go to a sports event, or go window shopping. You'll come back from your minivacation with renewed energy and courage.
8. Go jump in a hot bathtub. A hot bath or shower can do wonders for a shattered ego or harried nerves. (Unplug the phone, close the bathroom door, and relax.)

With this list of practical applications now intact, let us interrupt for some inspiration.

A Senseless Crime

Have you been committing any senseless crimes lately? That's a term I see in the newspaper every now and then. Frankly, I'm not sure what it means. If there is a sensible crime, I surely don't know what it is. But I think a senseless crime is one that doesn't seem to have any motive or meaning or will even do the criminal any good. Think about that for a minute while I tell you about Dr. Bob McCarthy.

This successful medical doctor from Hanover, Massachusetts, was a man that any of us could admire and even envy a little. He had it all: a thriving practice and the "good life" in a picturesque small town with a lovely wife and three beautiful daughters. He was respected in the community and appreciated by a long list of grateful patients.

But more than anything Dr. McCarthy seemed to have learned the secret of enjoying life. Every sunrise was the sound of trumpets to him, a new and precious day to be thankful for and to enjoy. Every hour was sixty precious minutes, and he didn't waste a tick of the clock. When he wasn't helping people feel better, he was romping through the Massachusetts woodlands with his young daughters. And at night, when many of his neighbors were lolling themselves into stupefaction in front of the TV, Dr. Bob was busy with projects, ideas, and activities.

Later he and his wife would lie awake and talk about how much they loved each other and the beautiful things of this world: art, music, literature. They were almost afraid to go to sleep in case they might miss a moment of living.

Well, it was not long until everyone around them knew why Dr. Bob had such a passion for living every precious moment. He didn't have many of them left, and he knew it. The leukemia in his blood was draining his strength, and in a matter of months he would be gone.

His life ebbed out less than two years after the disease

was diagnosed, but he lived more in his short life than many people do in the better part of a century. And he left us a lesson of how blessed is every breath we take—an understanding of the phrase *I don't have time.* The truth is that we have all the time there is!

Tho noxt timo you're tompted to commit a conceless crime, remember Dr. Bob McCarthy, because the senseless crime I'm talking about is *killing time!* As you kill and waste time you're keeping yourself from becoming all that you have the potential to become.

Think about what we're saying here. None of us knows if we are going to have a tomorrow, so we must take care of business today. We must stop killing time by competing against others, wishing we looked like others or trying to act like others. Our valuable time should be spent on something we can control—something realistic. Therefore, we must concentrate on controlling ourselves and use time wisely to do what we have to do when we have to do it. It also drives home this challenge point: *Don't just talk—do!* Saint Francis De Sales wrote, "Do not wish to be anything but what you are, and try to be that perfectly."

Piano Perfection

Ernest Saunders understands De Sales's statement and he lives by it. Ernest is a sixteen-year-old high school student from Philadelphia. He was taken by his music teacher to a scholarship audition at the world famous Settlement Music School. He took his place at the piano and began to play a complicated concerto. Suddenly Mrs. Evans, the school official, stood up and applauded and immediately awarded Ernest a full tuition-free scholarship. He was to enroll the next semester. Mrs. Evans was astounded at his ability and said his talent and playing grace were truly magnificent—unbelievable! With tears streaming down her cheeks, Mrs. Evans rushed forward to finish listening to Ernest brilliantly play the classical piece. Why? He was born with only one finger on his right hand.

Bernard Edmonds, the great American writer, clearly reiterates this inspirational message: "To dream anything that you want to dream. That is the beauty of the human mind. To do anything that you want to do. That is the strength of the human will. To trust yourself to test your limits! That is the courage to succeed."

As a final, concluding concept for this challenge, let us talk of Tunnel Vision.

Tunnel Vision Is Dangerous

As we plow the fields of life, many of us get too caught up in the obstacles and intensity of the moment and lose sight of the big picture. This is dangerous because it fertilizes the breeding ground of negativity, corruption, tunnel vision, depression, and discouragement.

Tunnel vision is when we think life is a linear plane— a straight line. We say to ourselves, "If things are going well they will always go well." This causes us to become complacent and lackadaisical in our efforts and we lose our competitive drive that got us on the success roll in the first place. This obviously is treacherous because life is not a linear plane.

What happens if we believe this linear philosophy and our progress tilts to the negative side? "If things are going wrong they will continue to go wrong." Now where does this straight-line philosophy lead to? We become depressed, lonely individuals with no hope or light at the end of the tunnel!

Again, life is not a linear plane. It's a circular plane! Life isn't a one-way street. It's a complete circle with high times and low times. Regardless of how successful people are at particular times in their lives, all of them have had

Figure 1

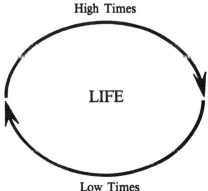

High Times

LIFE

Low Times

obstacles to overcome and challenging problems, heart-aches, and tragedy to deal with. The only reason they have become successful is because they have been willing to hang in there long enough. They have been patient and determined enough to grow from the negative emotional experiences and wait out the down times knowing the good times will roll again. Successful individuals everywhere, in every field of interest, prove that the time-honored virtues of hard work and perseverance really do work. Yes, what goes around comes around!

We need always to remember that everyone has been a failure and everyone has a past. So what's the big deal? We learn wisdom from failure much more than from success. If we have a negative experience and feel like a failure, we need to realize there is a difference between the person and the performance. You don't throw a guitar away just because it's out of tune. You don't throw the baby out with the dirty bath water! You are still a good person with more potential stuck inside of you, than you'll ever use in a lifetime, even if some of what you've done is bad. Your life is worthwhile and you still are a good person with constant opportunities to become better! Your contribution is still significant! We simply need to take the time to retune ourselves when we go off pitch.

Negative to Positive from

Negative to more Positive from. . .

If you have a negative experience, you can turn it into a positive experience by learning all you can from it. Therefore, it doesn't matter so much whether you win or lose, but what you learn!

And when the low times come again, as they definitely will in this circle of life, all we need to do is remember what caused the negative experiences and avoid the causes. As we learn from our tough times and stop making the same mistakes, eventually our low times don't last as long and each time we travel one revolution of this circle of success, we become better and better. Not that the circle gets larger or smaller—it remains the same—but the low times don't last as long and don't cut quite as deep. Therefore, it's a natural consequence that the good times will come more frequently and last longer.

Mistakes Are Great Teachers

History teaches us the kinds of pitfalls we will encounter. Therefore, avoid them. But if you fall, learn from them and forgive yourself. Then, forget your mistakes but never forget what they teach you! Great individuals, like tall trees, retain their stability during the most severe storms, so don't worry so much about stormy weather—just weather the storm!

Remember, there is something about the present: it doesn't last. So, if you do your best today and it isn't as good as you would have hoped, learn and evaluate and do it again and again if necessary. Never quit! Sometimes that's all it takes to complete the task—one more step and your dream comes true! And when times get really tough, as they sometimes will, still don't quit! Especially, don't give up and decide to end it all. We have to deal with life when we're alive, and we have to deal with death when we're dead!

Don't check out on momentary escapes such as alcohol and drugs. They only postpone our progress and stifle the chance for us to endure the down cycle, which allows the good times to roll! Remember George Weinberg's obser vation: "Giving up reinforces a sense of incompetence; going on gives you a commitment to succeed."

If you want to succeed and not just survive; if you want to win your share of the time; and, if you want to eliminate stress from your life, I suggest that you develop a new personal commitment to overcoming obstacles by constantly striving to be better than you've ever been before!

Remember, the greater the challenge, the more we excel. So, the next time you feel you've reached the edge and are about to fall off, remember that the world was made round!

I, Grandfather, challenge you to accept these philosophies and live by them. May the "force" be with you always as you weather the storm, and may you stay forever young! End of Challenge 8. Immediately go on to Challenge 9.

CHALLENGE 9

"There Ain't No Free Lunch"

Gilbert Arland said, "When an archer misses the mark, he turns and looks for the fault within himself. Failure to hit the bull's-eye is never the fault of the target. To improve your aim—improve yourself."

My Dad said, "There ain't no free lunch." These statements point out that we need to take personal responsibility for our own actions. When we do we will take notice of the consequences attached to the action and grow from each experience. If we make a mess and Mom cleans it up, who experiences the consequence of making a mess? Mom does, and this isn't right! We must be taught early that no matter what, we are responsible for the results of our actions. Our parents aren't responsible for our failure and success. Neither are our friends, our ethnic backgrounds, our teachers, our employers, our employees, or our neighborhood. Our government isn't responsible either! The only one responsible for you is you!

William Simon, former secretary of the United States Treasury said, "Half of Americans work for a living—the other half vote for it." Many politicians apparently understand this as they get votes by playing Santa Claus with the government's money!

I realize our schools are partly responsible for this "free lunch" attitude and warped value system. Every time a kid has trouble in a class or doesn't like a teacher, all he has to do is complain to the counselor and the class is changed! Teenagers today are not taught to take responsibility for their actions. And the problem escalates when they get out of high school and discover life isn't anything like what they're used to. There are no counselors around to cater to their likes and dislikes, and suddenly they are forced to cope with responsibility. If they refuse, they must pay the consequences. There is no "alternative school" or accommodating program to attend in real life! We must learn to behave and deal with our challenges head-on until we solve them! We must learn to succeed by society's rules, not by our own rules! That is how "real life" is always going to be.

Closed Minds Conceal The Light of Truth

If a little girl was walking along the top of a twenty-story building and fell off, what would happen to her? She would die just like you and I would. Even if she didn't understand the law of gravity, the law of gravity would affect her. Gravity doesn't change, so she has to change her behavior in order to survive. Earl Nightengale explains, "There are two general classes of people: those to whom their beliefs are more precious than the truth, even if truth should run contrary to their beliefs, and those to whom the truth is more precious than their beliefs. We meet both kinds of people in our daily lives. The first has a closed mind and they usually fail. The other an eager, open mind and they usually succeed." Which group do you fit in?

These two groups of believers become evident as we seek to find our philosophy of life and religion. William George Jordon wrote, "The man who has a certain religious belief and fears to discuss it, lest it be proved wrong, is not loyal to his beliefs; he has but a coward's faithfulness to his prejudices. If he were a lover of truth, he would be willing at any moment to surrender his belief for a higher, better, and truer faith."

This applies to each of us. And the higher principle in this case is learning to take personal responsibility for our own actions and believing "there ain't no free lunch!"

Before each of us was born, we were connected to our mothers with an umbilical cord—our lifeline. Through this cord we received every nourishment we needed to grow and prosper.

Nine months of luxury (except for the cramped quarters and poor lighting) later, the time came for us to move on. We were kicked out of the womb, our security blanket was taken away, and our umbilical cord was severed. We were on our own. Inside the womb we were given everything with or without asking. But now that we were outside, it was up to us to survive and get what we want. Sure, as young children all we had to do was cry about it and it was given, but we still had to go after what we wanted.

As time passed, however, the survival rules changed. In order for us to continue to succeed (the definition of success being getting what we want) we had to change. How many of us did? I know many individuals just as you do, who had their umbilical cords cut when they came into the world and are spending the rest of their lives trying to find another place to plug it back in! They still think all they have to do is cry and they will be given what they want. They feel the world owes them an easy living, automatic pay increases without an increase in productivity, more benefits with time off, and more pay for less work.

Hey, wait a minute! We are personally responsible for our own actions. We can't rely on someone else to give us what we want. We need to go after it ourselves! We need to develop the attitude that we will work so hard for what we want that if our employer won't give us a raise, somebody else will! Walpole wrote, "Men are often capable of greater things than they perform. They are sent into the world with bills of credit, and seldom draw to their full extent."

Too many individuals spend their whole lives waiting for their ship to come in, when in reality they never sent one out. If we wait for things to happen, they won't. Failure is not the worst thing in the world. The very worst is not to try. Therefore, the only time you can't afford to fail is the last time you try. So go ahead—go for it! Opportunity doesn't knock on anyone's door. You are opportunity— you open your own door! And you must be ready not only to take opportunities, but to make them.

Too many individuals try to make themselves feel good about their lack of success by attributing the success of others to luck. I know they don't realize it, but for once they are right! The true definition of luck is "the perfect moment when opportunity comes face to face with preparation." Gary Player said, "The harder you work the luckier you get." It's true. There ain't no free lunch! Today's preparation determines tomorrows achievement. We can only reap what we sow!

Nothing comes easy, but it will come! Not if we wait, but if we work!

The Kid Who Couldn't Talk

Do you ever feel as if you were one of nature's mistakes? An experiment that just didn't work out? The Edsel of the human race? That you have the brain of a Vegematic and a body like the Goodyear Blimp? I guess we've all had these feelings, and the next time you have them remember the story of this kid I'm about to tell you about. He had everything we've just said going for him: dumb, tongue-tied, fat, and ugly. He spent his academic life as he said, "in the lowest form of the lowest class of every school I attended."

Among other things, he couldn't talk straight. He stumbled and stammered and got his words and ideas all tangled together and generally made a mess of anything he said.

But he had one thing going for him—he knew he could do better. Nobody else seemed to care much, but he did. And when the class left him behind, he passed the time by reading the biographies of great men and women and by memorizing their sayings and thoughts in Bartlett's *Familiar Quotations*.

I'd like to tell you he lived happily ever after, but he didn't. He had a life of struggle, but he had at least one moment of superlative victory, when his imposing body, his iron will, and his magnificent golden phrases saved his homeland and perhaps the entire free world from being crushed under the iron-heeled boots of the Nazis.

He learned well from those great lives and great quotations, and he developed his own powerful way with words. During World War II he rallied his countrymen with some of the finest oratory the English language ever produced, including these words: "We will fight them on the airfields and on the beaches, and in the street we will never surrender. And if the empire lasts for a thousand years men will yet say this was their finest hour."

With such a leader before them how could the British help but be strong. They withstood, they won, and we will be forever grateful to the fat kid who couldn't talk but who grew up to become the prime minister of England and probably the greatest freedom fighter of this century—Winston Churchill. There ain't no free lunch! Freedom isn't a guaranteed gift—we must work and fight for it!

Land of Opportunity

Do you think America is still the land of opportunity?

Some people say the days of opportunity are past. But one of the people who is not saying this is Samuel Salter, Jr.

Samuel Salter, Jr., might have had cause to claim that America's doors of opportunity were now closed and bolted. After all, he lived in the old and settled eastern seaboard state of New Jersey. He was black, and historically in America blacks have had to struggle upstream to get a piece of the good life.

But Samuel Salter, Jr., was a man who saw obstacles in his path as stepping stones instead of stopping places. He didn't think much about what he didn't have. Instead, he concentrated on what he did have: a bright mind, enthusiasm, and a desire to help other people.

He took his bright mind and began to study finance and economics on his own. He devoured books. He dabbled in real estate as much as his limited funds would let him. And he planned and sketched out his future business. He offered his services. At first people were reluctant, but when they saw the quality of his work, the word soon spread and Samuel Salter, Jr., was soon a growing investment firm dealing in hundreds of thousands of dollars.

Up to now this is just another of the countless success stories in this great land of America. But there is one more detail that you may be particularly interested in. Samuel Salter, Jr., had another handicap: his lack of wrinkles. You see, while he was putting all this together, Samuel Salter, Jr., was still in high school!

If you want to do something great, don't think you need gray hair to do it! The choices you make today affect forever! There ain't no free lunch, but you can eat if you work hard!

Mouse in the House

Have you tripped over any golden opportunities lately?

It's easy to say, "Gee, if I just had more money or good looks or had more athletic ability, I'd be able to do this or that great thing." That's one way of looking at life and opportunities. But let me tell you the story of a man who saw life a little differently. Come back with me more than a half-century to a garage in the Midwest. Inside, a struggling, half-starved illustrator is trying to eke out a living with his illustrations. As he sits there straining for an inspirational idea, a mouse runs right across his foot.

Now mice are not particularly welcome in anybody's house, but in an illustrator's studio they are particularly obnoxious. They burrow into his papers, eat them, and shred them to make nests. They smell up the place, which doesn't add to the comfort of one with artistic sensibilities. And in the case of this poor artist, the presence of the mouse was just one more sign of his lack of success. To cap off the indignity, this wretched rodent didn't even have the decency to be afraid of him. It ran right over his foot without so much as a "beg your pardon."

The young illustrator watched that miserable mouse scurry back into the miserable wall. He stared at the miserable floor under him, the miserable ceiling above him, and thought about his miserable chances of success.

But then the difference between this man and many of us began to show itself. He began to imagine things in that pesky but perky mouse that most of us wouldn't think of. He envisioned a high squeaky voice, big ears, inquisitive eyes, and a pointed nose. By now his drawing hand was working feverishly over the paper and out came mouse friends, neighbors, and a long series of stories that haven't stopped yet.

America and the world have never been the same since that unknown mouse ran across that artist's foot, because the mouse soon got a name—Mickey. And the artist's name is tied to the happy childhood of people throughout the world, for he was the great Walt Disney.

So the next time you see a sign of failure crossing your path like a repulsive rodent, look again. It may be an opportunity trying to get your attention. There ain't no free lunch! But if you use your imagination to solve your problems, you will eventually succeed!!

Rolling Across America

Have you ever wanted to get away for awhile? Maybe take a nice long trip?

Michael King wanted to take a trip all across America, from Alaska to the Capitol in Washington, D.C. As many of us would feel, a trip across America's plains, up and down her rocky mountains, and through her mighty cities was an experience Michael wanted very much to have.

And so, like millions of other Americans, Michael saved his money, planned his trip, and set out. But Michael King's cross-country trip was a little different, and his reason for going was uniquely his own.

For one thing, his transportation was unique. He wore out four sets of wheels and went through fourteen pairs of gloves during the five months it took him to make the journey.

His reason? He said, "I wanted to show people they can fulfill their dreams, they can do anything they set their hearts on."

Michael King made his point. He generated thirty thousand dollars for handicapped centers across America. He also made a lot of us more determined to set out on our own journeys with faith and grit and determination.

You see, Michael King is paralyzed from the waist down, and he made that five-thousand-mile trip across America in his wheelchair. Michael understands there ain't no free lunch!

The Wisdom of Michael F. Wittowski

Would you like a little clue on how to be happy? Happiness, like love and self-esteem, can sometimes be a will-o'-the-wisp because the harder we chase it, the more it seems to escape us.

Let me share with you the wisdom of Michael F. Wittowski. He's not a Ph.D. or a college professor or a famous philosopher. He's kind of an average working guy and, as a matter of fact, that is the secret of his wisdom. He likes his job, he does it well, and he gets a kick out of contributing something good to society.

Too many of us get the idea that work is somehow a curse of the lower classes, when in reality doing good work is one of the best sources of happiness.

Mike Wittowski won some money awhile ago and was given the chance to quit his job. He said no; he was happy just to keep working. He said he would take the money he won, help his family a little bit, and give the rest away to a charity. He figured somebody could use it.

The money? It was a little more than picking up a few bucks at the factory football pool. Mike won the largest lottery in history—around forty million dollars. After winning, Michael still understands and firmly believes there ain't no free lunch!

Large Container—Large Reward

What are these stories leading to?

A wealthy man in South America called the locals to him one day and asked them to help him harvest his crop. He asked each of them to bring a container to help carry the crop to the market in town. At the end of the long and tiring work day, the man let each worker fill his container for himself as a wage. For those who had brought large containers it was a large and just payment compensation. But those who had purposely brought small containers so they wouldn't have to work as hard were disappointed when their compensation was small. Nevertheless, despite their complaints, their small wage was also just and fair!

This is a basic truth for success, whether it be in school, athletics, business, or home. We should seek nothing more than an honest day's pay in exchange for an honest day's work. "Vision without work is daydreaming and work without vision is drudgery." Regardless of who we are, how we look, the color of our skin, or where we grew up, the secret to happiness can be boiled down to a four-letter word: *work*! I realize this is an uncomfortable word to some, but work will help you feel fulfilled and worthwhile. Work will win when wishing won't! There definitely ain't no free lunch!

Let's learn to take personal responsibility for our own actions and our lives.

Responsibility for Oneself Reaps Rewards

W. Somerset Maugham said, "It's a funny thing about life: If you refuse to accept anything but the very best you will very often get it."

When we understand the simple truth of "there ain't no free lunch" and commit to making our dreams come true, we are ready to move on to the next level of instruction. Let me share an experience that proves these four statements true:

"Accept the challenges, so that you may feel the exhilaration of victory."—General Patton.

"Don't be afraid to take a big step if one is indicated. You can't cross a chasm in two small jumps."—David Lloyd George.

"The man who goes farthest is generally the one who is willing to do and dare."—Dale Carnegie.

"Act as though it were impossible to fail."—Paul Clark.

Hitchhiking in a Three-Piece Suit

I had just finished a speech at a business convention at the Holiday Inn in Fresno, California, and was preparing to return to the airport for a flight to my next engagement. My sponsors had treated me royally, including the use of a chauffeur-driven Cadillac limousine. With this in mind, I had no worries about taking my time packing my bags and saying farewell to my hosts. I knew I'd have plenty of time to catch my plane.

The chauffeur came to pick me and another gentleman up for the twenty-minute ride to the airport. She loaded the limo with our bags, opened the doors, helped us in, and off we went to catch our plane. Ten minutes into our drive, the car started to choke and jerk. The engine finally conked out and we coasted to a dead stop.

I looked at my watch. This couldn't be happening! We could miss our flight. The chauffeur turned around and looked at us sadly. "We have a problem. What are we going to do?" I replied, "No, we don't have a problem—*you* have a problem!" (It's a full-time job taking personal responsibility for my own problems without having to tackle others as well!) Now that I had her attention, I pointed out that our flight left precisely at 11:00 a.m. and it was now 10:40. We were still ten minutes from the airport. Again I inquired, "What are you going to do?" She replied, "I'll call on the radio for a taxi to come and get you." She called, and the taxi was on its way. We waited and waited and waited. I looked at my watch. We had been patiently waiting for two minutes now—definitely long enough! The gentleman riding with me looked at me and brought the situation into proper perspective. "What are *we* going to do?"

That was the key! I said, "Come on. Grab your bag." We got out of the limo, stood on the shoulder of the freeway, and with our suitcases at our feet, proudly and politely stuck out our thumbs. That's right! A sixty-one-year old, distinguished, upper-class, meticulously dressed gentleman in a five-hundred-dollar silk suit, and myself, also dressed in a nice suit, stood on the edge of the road and hitchhiked.

The very first car that came by screeched to a stop. (She was awesome!) We told the driver about our flight schedule and she said, "Hop in, let's go!" We scrambled into the tiny car, piled our luggage on our laps, and off we went. The driver "punched it" all the way to the airport and we made it just in time. We unraveled ourselves out of her small car, gave her five dollars for gas, thanked her and raced to the departure gate. And . . . we caught our plane!

This is a perfect example of everyday situational life. In every instance, we can either choose to wait for things to happen (in which case they may never happen) or we can take the initiative and make things happen. It is a choice, and the choice is ours!

As we have discussed before, making things happen by taking personal responsibility for our own actions is a basic ingredient for success. Dr. H. Stephen Glen in his remarkable book, *Developing Capable People,* writes that learning to take responsibility implies that we can relate the consequences of our behavior to the decisions we make and the actions we take. In other words, we don't just sit there, we do! We look at each situation and figure out what behavior best fits our circumstances, and then we adapt to the situation to get positive results. Through this, we don't lose our identity or integrity, and our values remain the same.

We Stereotype Ourselves

There are several ways to act in any situation, and we need to decide which is the most proper response. When someone buys you jewelry, is it appropriate for you to bring up the cost? Of course not! That would spoil the gift. Instead, you hug and kiss the giver—a very appropriate response.

Can most people adapt? I don't think so. It's not that they can't, but they refuse to. How can we tell if someone is set in his or her ways? Just listen to them! For example, how many times do we hear the line, "So, tell me a little about yourself" when we meet someone for the first time? And how many times is the response, "I'm the type of person who . . ."? This person is sending a loud, clear message: "I refuse to adapt. No matter what happens I will always be like this or that." They refuse to accept the consequences of their behavior and are always blaming the system. People like this always claim they are victims of circumstance. Instead of taking responsibility for their actions, they blame their bad behavior on someone or something else. "The system didn't accept me," "The computer made the error," "Management wasn't on the ball," "The light was bad," "I had no time to prepare," "The New York office changed its mind." Excuses, excuses, excuses! No one wants to listen to that.

We must be willing to change and adapt! If we don't, we'll never make it when we get our big break to meet with an important educator, coach, business person, or politician. Refusing to adapt means we say inappropriate things like, "I'm just going to be me. Why should I stop swearing and change my torn-up pants, cut my hair and put on shoes for this interview? This is me, and if he can't accept me for the way I am, that's tough. You and your system can just bite the wall!"

Does this sound familiar? Do you know someone like this who refuses to conform and somewhat play the game of society survival? Individuals who fit into this personality mold need to change. And if they refuse to change, who's fault is it? The simple success principle involved here is that to obtain or achieve a specific result we must exercise the appropriate behavior. To change and acquire the appropriate behavior, we must change our attitude. Attitude changes behavior; behavior gets results.

You see, we can change and be exactly who we need to be! And change doesn't imply weakness—it means nothing more than self-improvement. It implies good perception and a conscientious effort to succeed.

How can we learn to adapt? By ceasing to label everything that happens to us. We must avoid the "paralysis of analysis!" Labels become catchalls for everything—*burnout, stress, depression, jet lag, that time of month, a sign of the zodiac, the devil made me do it!* The bottom line is this: It doesn't matter what these experiences are called! Instead of wasting so much time discussing them and itemizing their symptoms, just adapt to every situation so it won't eat at you. We have the innate ability to do what's necessary to get us through our stress if we don't sit there and worry and complain or blame someone else for what is happening. Let us simply say to ourselves, "Regardless of whose fault it is, I'm taking personal responsibility for me and I'm going to do what's necessary to solve this dilemma." Then overcome your fear by doing whatever you fear. Overcome your stress by taking the steps necessary to change it. I guarantee that this tactic works! The secret is to keep your eye on the destination and believe that the end result is worth the hassle.

I wish you could come with me on the road for one week. A typical day presents several different situations that force one to learn to adapt. I fly more than 150,000 miles and give more than 300 speeches a year. And, believe it or not, I have never missed a speech! Please come with me for a quickie course in stress management, jet lag, and rising to the occasion.

A Knock on the Airplane Door

One day, I left Memphis, Tennessee, on an airplane (which is generally the way I fly!) to Minneapolis, Minnesota, to catch another plane to Denver, Colorado, so I could rent a car and drive an hour and a half to make a speech that evening at 8:00 p.m.

We were all aboard the jet in Memphis and beginning to accelerate to take off. The plane was speeding down the runway when suddenly, the pilot slammed on the brakes. The cargo door had opened. Needless to say we turned around and pulled into the gate area for repairs.

How long would it take? I didn't feel pressure but I did calculate the latest possible departure time in order to catch the next airplane to Minneapolis. After a while, I got nervous. But, as I sat there, it dawned on me. Why was

I fretting? I had no reason to worry because there was nothing I could do to change the situation. Why worry about something I had no control over? The definition of worry is *not making a decision.* The decision had been made for me! (Anyway, my only choice was to hijack the plane, and I couldn't do that!)

Finally the door was repaired and we took off for Minneapolis. As soon as we landed, I was up in the aisle. Before the plane could stop I grabbed my carry-on shoulder bag, my briefcase, and a box of movies. Over the loudspeaker, the flight attendant warned, "Please be seated; the plane hasn't stopped yet." I leaned on the seat!

The second the plane stopped and the door opened, out I shot. I mean I bolted out, down the jetway (the portable walkway that allows us to walk from the terminal directly on the plane) and out into the terminal, asked the attendant which gate my flight was leaving from, and listened for the answer as I flew in the appropriate direction.

I was "smokin' " down the concourse, dodging wheelchairs, hurtling benches, and throwing moves on people you wouldn't believe! Little kids were chasing me yelling, "O.J. Simpson, O.J. Simpson!!" I got to the gate, ran down a twenty-yard ramp, grabbed the knob of the closed door and yanked. It wouldn't budge. I could see the plane through the window, so I jerked at it again. The door was locked. A few yards away, an airline employee yelled to me, "You can't go through there. The door is locked." I thought, "No kidding! Who is this guy, a genius? Of course it's locked!"

I yelled back, "I know it's locked, but I'm on that plane." He said, "No, you're not!" I said, "I'm supposed to be. Please open the door!"

In his little squeaky voice he said, "It's too late." I roared, "No it's not! The plane is right there. Please get over here and open this door!" (I have always believed the best policy is to never say no when you can say yes. It's never too late if there's still one little, tiny, small chance!) He quickly opened the door.

I ran through the door, and raced down the jetway. When I got to the end, wouldn't you know it, it had already been pulled away from the airplane. There I stood, with four feet of space between me and the plane and twenty feet straight down. And to top it off, the airplane door was shut and locked.

Now what? I had only one choice. I put down my carry-on bags, held on to the vertical metal bar on the end of the jetway, leaned out toward the plane, stretched as far as I could and pounded on the airplane door. Now if you were inside the plane with the door locked and you heard a knock on the door, what would you do?

The flight attendant surprisingly inquired through the door, "Who is it?" I laughed and replied, "I'm on this plane!" She said with a chuckle, "Oh no, you're not." I said, "I'm supposed to be; open the door!" What would you do? She opened the door!

By this time the airline terminal employee had caught up to me and said, "Hold on while I move the jetway closer." He pushed the button and we moved forward to connect with the plane. The airplane door opened, and, totally out of breath, I climbed aboard. We took off, and I arrived in Denver, rented the last available car, sped up the mountain and delivered my speech. See, we can adapt! What's the big deal?!

I share this story not only to demonstrate the importance of learning to adapt, but to put to rest any *jet lag, burn out,* or *it-was-out-of-my-control* excuses. In the preceding week and a half, I had already spoken in San Francisco; Toronto, Canada; Utah; Chicago; Miami; Las Vegas; Anaheim, California; and Memphis, Tennessee. And in that order! And to top it off, during this exciting ten days I lost my wallet in Chicago and didn't have any checks, credit cards, or cash with me for the middle three days of this trip. Sure, I felt stress, but I didn't let it get me down.

We can't eliminate stress and anxiety and negative experiences, but we can learn to manage them. Herein lies the key! Accept the situation at face value and take it head-on and do what needs to be done. There is always a positive solution. We never have to give up. Where there's a will there's always a way! We just need to find it! I didn't experience jet lag or stress because I didn't take my eye off the goal. I willingly paid the price today so I could enjoy the rewards forever. I didn't get caught up in that stressful situation because I knew that the end result was well worth all of my extra efforts.

I challenge you to stop analyzing yourself so much, to stop worrying so much about what may happen, and concentrate on what *is* happening. Then simply do what needs to be done, when and where it needs to be done! Don't label negative emotions with titles to be used later as excuses. Rather, concentrate on developing a positive attitude that things can only get better! Commit to doing your part. Take personal responsibility for your desired results and accomplishments. Then, simply do it! Perhaps the word *now* is an appropriate conclusion.

I, Grandfather, challenge you to accept this philosophy and live by it. May the "force" be with you always as you weather the storm, and may you stay forever young! End of Challenge 9.

After carefully reading through and rereading through challenges 8 and 9, I came to realize that every challenge in the sacred book as well as every challenge and situation in everyday life simply boils down to *personal responsibility.* "Stuff" truly does happen, but the only thing we are not in charge of is whether or not we are in charge! Grandfather is absolutely right: everyone—each and every single one of us—can weather the storm if we want to badly enough! This immediately caused me to wonder about service. My whole life, I've heard the phrase "serve others." What is it? Why should I? How does it work? I wondered how it affected goals and my ability to satisfy my personal needs.

I guessed it was time to move ahead and study Challenge 10.

I've been shocked for several days now, as I have reread and relived my amazing dream. It was now clear to me that the "force" was with me—that focusing on reality causes energy. I still don't know if the dream experience was real or imagined, but it definitely had an impact on my destiny. The lessons of the dream have changed my life into a constant search for personal peak performance! I know I was born to win and I'm going to do it!!

I quickly turned to read challenge 10. To my surprise it simply said, "Life is a big storybook made up of little stories. You are writing your own book of life full of your experiences. You are the sum total of your past experiences. Now that the 'force' is with you, take the necessary time to reflect back on your life and write out challenge 10 on your own. Generations to come will benefit from your wisdom, knowledge, and understanding. The challenge is: If you had one day to live, what would you do differently? What would you focus in on? What would you want others to remember you by? What is more valuable to know than anything else you can think of? What message will you now leave behind? Record it here in this sacred book and call it challenge 10."

CHALLENGE 10

Service: The Name of the Game

Emerson wrote, "If you find life is empty, try putting something into it. Kindness is the language that the deaf can hear and the blind can see. You cannot do a kindness too soon because you never know how soon it will be too late."

Earl Campbell, the great NFL fullback, said, "Somebody will always break your records. It is how you live that counts." O.J. Simpson elaborates on this: "Fame is a vapor, popularity is an accident, money takes wings. Those who cheer you today may curse you tomorrow. The only thing that endures is character and what we've done for others."

If only we could live twice. If only we could live once and experience trial and error, victory and defeat, and be granted the memory of all our experiences when we live again. Then, when we relived every experience, we would have the retrospective knowledge of why we won or lost and be able to avoid pitfalls and maximize the positive results.

How many times do we catch ourselves saying, "If only I had known then what I know now," or "If only I could do that again, things would now be so different." Most of us have regrets and wish we could reenact many of our life's situations that are now history. But we know we can't. However, if we learn from others who have gone before us, who have experienced what we are now experiencing, we can in a sense live a retrospective life. When we learn from others, we don't have to experiment in our own lives.

Running Out of Time

Life is short and time is valuable. So what better knowledge of the worthwhile expenditure of time can we gain than from one who is running out of time?

On December 27, 1984, my father celebrated his sixty-seventh birthday. He stood at our family dinner and expressed his love for his wife and children, said he felt great, and shared some of his goals and dreams he had set for the next twenty years of his life.

On January 1, 1985, he fell over in excruciating pain. He was rushed to the hospital, and the next morning the doctors operated. When they opened him up, the doctors discovered my father was filled with cancer. They removed half of his small intestine and sewed him back up. The doctors explained the cancer and declared it too widespread for any successful treatment. They gave my dad six months to live.

Here is a man, my dad, who planned and dreamed just as each of us do. Who believed as we all do that it will always happen to the other guy, that we have plenty of time to do things later.

We must avoid procrastination! I wish you could talk to my dad each day as I do. It's been more than four years since his operation and he looks at each day as a bonus. He definitely has an increased sense of urgency, a quicker step, and increased productivity. He crams more into one day than most of us fit into a week—maybe a lifetime! He understands what it means to have a deadline.

Watching my dad reminds me of a professional basketball game. They should just give each team 100 points and let them play the last two minutes of the game. Why? Because more happens in the last two minutes of the game than happens during the rest of it! Why? Because there is a deadline. Every coach and every player knows when time will run out, so they suddenly surge with energy. They make adjustments and scramble to win. My father feels the same way and is also trying to scramble and accomplish that little bit more. The best part of this story is that my father has lived such a successful, highly productive life already that one wouldn't think he would have to make up for lost time. But he just keeps working because he wants to go out with his boots on. He has never lived as if there was plenty of time, but what if he had? How would he feel now?

I share my dad's predicament with you to remind you of reality. Each of us is born to die. How many years it takes, no one knows. We don't know if we'll even make it until tomorrow. No one knows the day of his death. Are you ready?

Not are you ready to die, but are you ready to live? If we don't know if we'll see tomorrow, we better live today! And we better do something that will be of worth, something that will outlast us. We must dedicate ourselves to something bigger than ourselves.

Ask yourself, What do I want to have written on my gravestone? How do I want to be remembered? Who will remember me and mourn my passing? I can't take anything with me except my education, so what am I leaving behind? The second we die someone else will own everything we've worked so hard to obtain.

I interviewed my father, and he is the one who asked me these questions. He is the one who literally showed me the single most important activity we can spend our time on—service. At this writing, his seventy-one years reveal a lifetime of love and service to his fellow man.

Service (with a capital *S*) is the name of my father's game and the name of the game of happy, rewarding, successful living.

Everyone who knows my dad has at least one or two stories about his unwavering service to his fellow man. His reputation is a noble one! One of my favorites is an experience I shared with him.

Circus Service

When I was a teenager, my father and I were standing in line to buy some tickets for the circus. Finally there was only one family between us and the ticket counter. This family made a big impression on me. There were eight children, all probably under the age of twelve. You could tell they didn't have a lot of money. Their clothes were not expensive clothes, but they were clean. The children were very well behaved, all of them standing in line, two-by-two, behind their parents, holding hands. They were excitedly jabbering about the clowns, elephants, and other acts they would see. One could sense they had never been to the circus before. It promised to be a highlight of their young lives.

The father and the mother were at the head of the pack standing proud as could be. The mother was holding her husband's hand, looking up at him as if to say, "You're my knight in shining armor." He was looking at her as if to reply, "You got that right!"

The ticket lady asked the father how many tickets he wanted. He proudly responded, "Please let me buy eight children's tickets and two adult tickets so I can take my family to the circus."

The ticket lady quoted the price.

The man's wife let go of his hand—her head dropped— the man's lip began to quiver. The father leaned a little closer and again asked, "How much did you say?"

The ticket lady again quoted the price.

The man didn't have enough money.

How was he supposed to turn and tell his eight kidlets that he didn't have enough money to take them to the circus?

Seeing what was going on, my dad put his hand into his pocket, pulled out a twenty-dollar bill, and dropped it on the ground. (We were not wealthy in any sense of the word!) My father reached down, picked up the bill, tapped the man on the shoulder, and said, "Excuse me, sir, this fell out of your pocket."

The man looked straight into my dad's eyes, took my dad's hand in both of his, and with his lip quivering and a tear streaming down his cheek, he replied, "Thank you, thank you, sir, this really means a lot to me and my family."

My father and I went back to our car and drove home. We didn't go to the circus that night, but we didn't go without. Following his next payday, we did get to the circus. So what is the message?

The message here is service. That man never got my father's name, but it didn't matter. My father's goal was simply to be of service, not to reap glory.

I have a wealthy uncle. He would have accomplished the same goal, but he would have wanted the glory. He would've said to the distraught father, "What, you can't afford to go to the circus? No problem, it's on me! In fact, stop that bus, let me take the whole neighborhood. I'll write the check now!"

Sure, my uncle would have accomplished the same goal, but he would have wanted the credit. Is this true, unselfish service? Of course not! True service is doing a deed when you may not get the glory. It's living the philosophy that it's not who's right but what's right that counts!

My father not only provided financial service when the father wasn't looking for it, but more important, he also provided pride service (allowing the man to save face), family togetherness service, and love service.

Quiet, unselfish service is what we'll be remembered for when we die. It is the most noble expenditure of time we can involve ourselves in.

Teaching: A Universal Vocation

Service comes in many forms. Probably the most notable form is found in the teaching profession. Grandfather obviously taught everyone this! We can be parents teaching at home or in line to purchase circus tickets (my experience with my dad taught me about service), students helping fellow students, a coach going out of his way to assist a player in practice, or a corporate executive walking side by side with a hard-working employee. Regardless of the role, the result is the same. The willingness to teach and unselfishly serve is the most noble calling in life. Without teachers, no one would ever progress or reach his or her capacity for greatness.

As each of us reflects on our lives and on the lives of those who have been of greatest service to us, I'm sure we'll remember our school days. We can all remember two or three teachers who have affected our lives, who really understood the significance of their calling. They didn't just teach math or English or P.E., they taught students. They truly understood the meaning of unselfish service. As a testimonial to those teachers who truly serve and are committed to making a difference, I relay the following story.

When I was a sophomore in high school, I was a typical kid. I was going through the stage when I thought I knew more than my parents. It was all I could do to let them live at my house!

I was tall and so skinny that I had to jump around in the shower to get wet! I didn't have a lot of friends and hadn't yet quite caught the vision of the importance of academics. The only reason I went to school was to stay eligible for athletic competition.

As I look back, I realize that this stage of life brings a need for a healthy, supplement-to-parent relationship. This relationship is defined as "Every good parent needs a good teacher, and every good teacher needs a good parent." To help a student really succeed, efforts of both parents and teachers must complement each other.

I was lucky enough to have had one such teacher who truly understood service and who made a significant difference in my young life.

Several weeks into the school year, I met Mr. Croft, the anthropology teacher. I didn't know much about anthropology then and I still don't know much about it, therefore, I never signed up for any of his classes. However, Mr. Croft really sensed my need and decided to go the extra mile. He knew what a difference he could make in my insecure life if he just put out a little bit of extra effort. Consequently, he and I became good friends.

Every morning at 8:15, Mr. Croft would be standing in the doorway of his classroom, ready to greet me. He always made me feel as if it was by accident. But as I look back on it now, I know he purposefully planned this rendezvous each morning because he understood that shy, insecure, lonely Danny Clark needed a friend and a boost for the day.

My first class was on the other side of the building. But, because Mr. Croft always made me feel I was special, I was always late for my first-period class to detour by his room. It was worth getting in trouble for! I couldn't afford to miss his pep talk each day. He put positive-thinking gas in my tank!

After our conversation I would literally float through school convinced that I was somebody and that I could do things just like everyone else! I knew I was important and that I could and should work hard and contribute to my family, to my community, to my class, to my teams, and to the school.

I'm sure you agree that we never forget great individuals like Mr. Croft. But how can we possibly repay them?

A Favor Repaid

I had been out of high school a few years when I had an opportunity to go back to my old stomping grounds to coach little league football. My team consisted of the thirteen-year-old boys. I didn't know any of these young men, so on the first day of practice I put them into two equal lines and started throwing the ball to them. I was trying to formulate a team in my mind as I watched them run, catch, and throw.

Two-and-a-half days into practice, onto the field walked a tall, skinny kid. He reminded me of me when I was his age. He had come straight from school and had on a pair of brand-new pants, a new shirt, and new dress shoes. I stopped him and asked, "Can I help you?"

He replied, "Yeah, coach, I want to play football."

I replied, "Great, but don't you want to go home and change your clothes like the other guys have done?"

He replied, "Well, coach, I've already missed two days of practice and I didn't want to miss anymore. Is it okay if I stay?"

I thought this was pretty cool and said, "Sure, get in line to go out for a pass."

It finally came time for him to go out for his pass. I dropped back and threw the ball to him the best I could. It hit him square in the side of the face. He raced over to the ball, picked it up, and ran it straight back to me. When any of the other players had missed the ball, they would stomp around and throw the ball back to me, making me run for it! This shy, skinny kid was different.

It came time for him to go out for his second pass. I dropped back and threw the ball as best I could, giving him every chance to catch it. It hit him square in the other side of his head. (This poor guy couldn't catch a cold, much less a football!) His nose was now bleeding, but he raced over, picked up the ball, and ran it back to me. As he got back in line, I thought, "Man, he is amazing!" It came time for him to go out for his third pass. I really wanted him to catch this one so I threw it easy. But I threw it too far out in front of him. Wouldn't you know it? He dove for the ball, missing it and skidding over the grass. He got up, grass-stained from head to toe, picked the mud from his clothes, held his pocket which was ripped, raced to the ball, picked it up, and ran it back to me! I decided I better have a talk with him before he killed himself! There had to be something else besides football that he could spend his energy on.

I gave the ball to one of the players so he could continue the catching drill and pulled this guy out of line. I said, "We've got to have a talk. Why are you out here? Does your dad want a football star for a son? Are you out here because your friends want you to play?" I'll never forget his response.

He looked up at me with sparkling eyes and replied, "Coach, I'm out here because I really want to play football. And I promise if you'll help me, I know I can do it!"

I was touched by his sincerity and determination and asked what his name was. He answered, "My name is Tommy Croft."

A light went on inside my head. I asked, "Does your dad teach anthropology at East High School?"

He answered, "Yes, he does."

I said, "Get back in line!" Here was my chance to be a Mr. Croft to a Croft! Here was my chance to be of service and to make a difference in a young man's life. Here was my chance to put something back into the system that I had taken out of for so many years. Here was my chance to finally understand what my grandfather, father, and Mr. Croft had been teaching me: What goes around comes around.

Service truly is the name of the game of life. It's what

we should want to be remembered for after we're gone. This is probably why you're a devoted friend, a caring parent, a dedicated coach, an empathetic employer, a conscientious employee, or a professional educator. Each of us wants to make a difference and leave a legacy behind.

As a tribute to my father and his lessons of service that he has taught me and in recognition of the unselfish service that Mr. Croft and other teachers, coaches, parents, student leaders, employers, employees, and school administrators have had on my life, I wrote this song. It's recorded on my first album, *The Best Is Yet to Be*. I dedicate it to all of them!

Quiet Heroes

The world is full of quiet heroes
Who never seek the praise
They're always back off in the shadows
They let us have the limelight days.

For this you're the one that I look up to
Because of you I'm free
You set an example I could follow
You helped me see my destiny

So even though my thanks don't show
Unnoticed you will never go
I need to say I love you so
You're my hero!

I've had my share of broken dreams
But you said I could win
You gave me the chance I always needed
To start my dreams again

You took the time to teach and tutor
You showed me rules to rise
You changed my fears to glory tears
You're an angel in disguise.

So even though my thanks don't show
Unnoticed you will never go
I need to say I love you so
You're my hero!

I wouldn't be where I am today
I've won my share of times
Unless you coached me through the maze
And pushed me on the hardest climbs

It's just your style, the extra mile
"No glory" must be tough
You let me have the accolades
A smile you said was just enough.

So even though my thanks don't show
Unnoticed you will never go
I need to say I love you so
You're my hero!

It's true. You are someone's hero, someone's quiet hero. If you're not, you could be, you should be! And all of your hard work, all of your sacrifice, preparation, and seemingly unnoticed service will all be worthwhile if you help but one child.

But you ask, "Is all the time and effort worthwhile for one child?" Definitely yes! What if that one child were yours?

Remember the crucial importance of service. Our service to others is the rent we pay for our room on this earth. I challenge all of us to pay our bills and to ponder, "Man cannot always see rightly with the eyes. For what is important is hidden within the heart."

The Risks of Service Bring Great Rewards

Shakespeare wrote, " 'Tis not enough to help the feeble up, but to support him after."

We have established that to teach is to serve. Let's take it one step further. To be of service means that the server is willing to take a risk.

The "Risks" of Service

To laugh is to risk appearing to fool.
To weep is to risk appearing sentimental.

To reach out for another is to risk involvement.
To expose feelings is to risk exposing your true self.
To place your ideas, your dreams before the crowd is to risk
their loss.
To love is to risk not being loved in return.
To live is to risk dying.
To try is to risk failure.
To serve is to risk not being appreciated.

As threatening and uncomfortable as they may seem, risks must be taken. Life's greatest hazard is to risk nothing. The person who risks nothing does nothing, has nothing, and is nothing. He may avoid suffering and sorrow, but he simply cannot learn, feel, change, grow, love or live! Chained by his fears, he is a slave, he has forfeited freedom. Only a person who risks is free. Free to feel good about himself and become the best he can be so he can give of himself to others. This is how we learn to serve and become effective people builders. It involves risking *personal touch.*

Even though our society has changed from the agricultural economy of 150 years ago to the industrial economy of 80 years ago and now to an informational economy, one thing hasn't changed: People will be more productive if they're treated like people. This personal touch theory is based on the premise that technology has been over-emphasized during the industrial-technical age, while people have not been emphasized enough. Business owners, managers, and educators have forgotten some of the basics about interaction with people.

Pay is not a motivator. Studies show it's a temporary motivator but soon is taken for granted. It's the personal touch and relationship that provides the best rewards for most people. And studies show that happy people, those who enjoy their associates, are more excited about work. Excitement increases their creativity, improves their memory, and accelerates their productivity.

Spaced repetition is the best learning tool, so let's review. We have just gone full circle. To teach effectively is to serve. To be of service is to risk. One major risk is to open up and genuinely communicate with your associates. The best way to do this is the personal touch theory—treating people as if they were people. It's accomplished with the understanding that it's ok to develop a friendship and relationship with those with whom you work and teach, because only then can you really teach and really serve— and this circle begins again.

There are two other powerful circles we should evaluate that more deeply explain the concepts of human touch, feeling, and service. They reiterate the importance of getting our own lives in order before we can effectively teach information to others.

Two Powerful Circles

In most ways our feelings about ourselves make us the kind of persons we are. When I feel that I am healthy, worthwhile, and productive, I then spend less energy on myself and my own problems. It is a powerful circle: I love myself, which permits me the freedom to turn outward toward others. When I do this, responses of love and interest are directed to me from others, and these responses make me feel even more secure and worthwhile.

Figure 2
Basic Feelings of Self-Worth

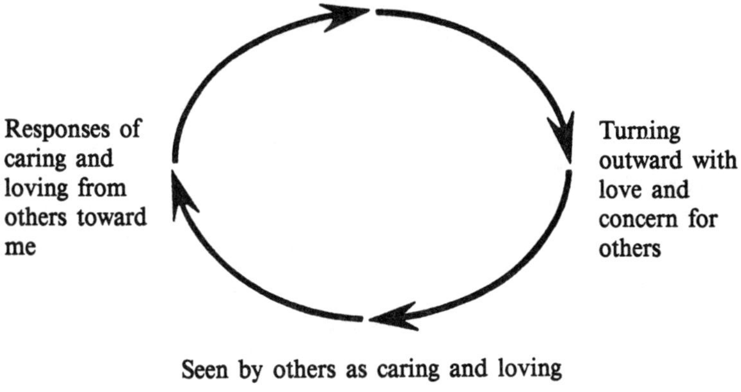

Responses of caring and loving from others toward me

Turning outward with love and concern for others

Seen by others as caring and loving

On the other hand, when I dislike myself, I spend an inordinate amount of time concerned with myself. I am turned inward. This also has an effect on others. I am probably seen as an egocentric, selfish person who cares only for himself. When I am in this state, the messages I receive from others are largely negative.

These negative messages strengthen my original unpleasant feelings about myself. How can we break the second circle and change it so that it becomes more like the first? How can we increase our own sense of worth? It's easy! We just increase the amount of service we render to our fellow men. Everything boils down to unselfish service.

Before we move on, let's take a moment to reflect on these two circle philosophies and prepare a self-audit. Let's do a little soul-searching to see if we are currently mentally and emotionally prepared to teach and be of service. Ask yourself: Would I like to live with myself? Would I like to work for myself? If I were choosing someone I had to trust, could I trust me? Would I like to meet myself if I were in trouble? Would I like to be at my own mercy? Would I want a neighbor, parent, teacher, or employer to be just like me? Would I want a child to be exactly like me?

Figure 3
Basic Feelings of Unworthiness

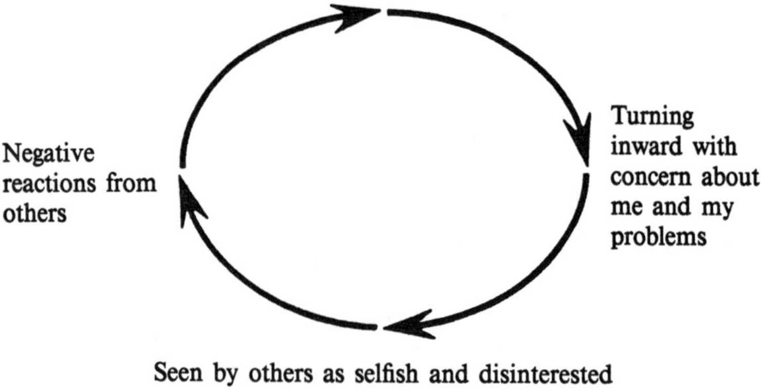

Negative reactions from others

Turning inward with concern about me and my problems

Seen by others as selfish and disinterested

I've been lucky to have been exposed to certain individuals who did stack up to these ideals, and they stacked up high! They had their lives in order and were able to pass along success principles to help others get their lives together

My mother is a classic example of one who has always been of service no matter what is going right or wrong in her life. No matter how much she wants to do and have for herself, she is always willing to totally sacrifice for her family and friends. She willingly goes without sleep and fame and glory just to assist her family and friends. Sure, my mother has had many struggles and setbacks in her productive life, but she has continued to serve others. Why? Because she believes WGACA! Yes, great leaders and friends echo my grandfather, Mr. Croft, my father, my mother, my K.C., and every other unselfish human being who understands that it is better to give than to receive.

This "golden rule" philosophy is important for all of us who are interested in the joys that come from teaching, coaching, leading, and serving. For what goes out eventually comes back to us. When we help and serve just one person, our influence and service can travel far. In fact, sometimes we'll never know when a simple word, a look, or a touch from us will be the turning point in someone else's life. It may even be a turning point in our own life. Yes, one person serving others does, can, and will make a difference.

Service builds character, develops teamwork, spawns support, boosts morale, and satisfies our individual needs to feel loved, wanted, important, and secure. Everyone has the capacity to serve. We only need a worthy cause to believe in. And when we find the right cause, our abilities and actions always catch up! Service is the fundamental ingredient for successful living. Through service we learn about motivation, commitment, organization, following through, risk-taking and love. If you think about it, everything good in life comes out of unselfish service.

I've seen service projects build self-esteem and a strong

self-worth, change people from troublemakers to trouble-shooters, improve reputations, unite schools, strengthen families, and save corporations. Real, meaningful service truly is the key to the kingdom of inner peace and happiness. I'm sure you'll agree as I share the following experience.

Wild Man "Makes a Difference"

I travel from coast to coast each year and speak to groups ranging from top-level corporate management to teachers in service to students in high school and middle school. Like every business, every school also has at least one or two negative individuals who tear others down. Sadly, these negative individuals are sometimes teachers who sit in the faculty lounge and talk badly about a specific student. They label him as the "good-for-nothing troublemaker" and the cancerous bad reputation soon spreads throughout the school.

I visited one such high school with a faculty lounge that had a typical conversation going on about "Wild Man" (I didn't know his name)—the typical, insensitive showoff who would never amount to much. One teacher was so upset at him, she finally blurted, "This dope-smokin', frisbie-throwin', bicycle-ridin', flag-burnin', long-haired hippie should be shot! And I hear he has brothers!"

I got tired of listening to the gossip (gossiping is a sign that the gossiper is insecure) so I left and went into the auditorium to test out the sound system prior to the start of my assembly program. There, I met the positive principal and the activities director who filled me in on the purpose of the day.

About a month before, a young man in the school—a friend to everyone, was beginning to face a dilemma. He had multiple sclerosis—a nerve disease that affects the muscles of the body. He had a manual wheelchair to propel himself around the halls, but it was suddenly not enough.

His disease had progressed to the point where he could no longer get around. His only choices were to either buy an electric wheelchair or to check out of school and attend a school for the handicapped. His family was poor and couldn't afford the price of the required electric wheelchair, so he was forced to check out of school.

Today, the day I was at school, was the day he was leaving. His parents were at school in the counselor's office filling out the paperwork. Neither the boy nor his parents were aware of what was going on. In fact, most of the teachers and students didn't even know! The principal announced the assembly and excused the school to go to the auditorium.

Before I was to speak, that day's assembly would be presentation day. The principal introduced the student body president. She went through a few formalities and suddenly introduced "Wild Man"—the student the teachers were talking so negatively about in the teachers' lounge. The second he touched the microphone, all the teachers thought World War III had just started! What was "Wild Man" doing on stage?!

As "Wild Man" gave the cues, four football players got up and walked over to the young man in his wheelchair. He and his parents had just come into the auditorium and they were sitting in the aisle at about the fifteenth row. The football players lifted him out of the chair and carried him up onto the stage. "Wild Man" gave another cue to two band members. They in turn, presented the kid's parents with flowers and escorted them up to the stage to be with their son. "Wild Man" momentarily left the stage but soon returned driving a brand new shiny, chrome-plated electric wheelchair with a giant red-and-white (the school colors) bow on it. The football players lowered the boy with MS into the chair, showed him how to operate it, and stepped back to let everyone see him make two victory laps around the stage. There wasn't a dry eye in the house as we all stood up simultaneously and gave

"Wild Man" and the "wheelchair kid" a five-minute standing ovation.

What had happened? Thirty days before this assembly—the day the student with MS found out he couldn't afford an electric wheelchair, "Wild Man" caught wind of it. Under his own initiative, he rallied five of his "wild" friends and together they started their own fund-raiser. They collected aluminum cans and turned them in for cash refunds. "Wild Man" and his so-called good-for-nothing friends raised enough money to purchase the wheelchair themselves. "Wild Man" had help from other students in service organizations like Key Club and the student council, but he organized it and followed through!

Now what do you think? Can one person make a difference? Is service the secret to love, to motivation, to togetherness? Is service a vehicle to break down our social barriers and escalate our leadership qualities? Yes, service is the beginning and the end of successful living and the key ingredient in our pursuit of happiness! It makes bad people good, good people great, and great people better than ever before! One man—one so-called wild man brought down the social stereotypical class walls and at the same time brought up the school and made them one! Decide today to risk success in the service of your fellow men. It's the only thing that will bring about racial equality and world peace. The far-reaching and long-lasting benefits and personal feelings of worth that accompany unselfish service far exceed anything life has to offer. Let us serve one another and once and for all remember WGACA!

I, Daniel, under the direction of Grandfather and by the power of the great Kahuna, challenge you to accept this most important challenge and live by it. May the "force" be with us always as we weather the storm, and may we all stay forever young. End of challenge 10.

* * *

After having decided that the most important message is *service*, the "force" made it clear to me why the other challenges needed to come before challenge 10. We must first take care of ourselves, learn to like and love ourselves, and become successful in our own right before we can ever find the time and motivation to serve others. And when we do, everyone benefits and the whole world smiles.

With this understanding that we must strengthen ourselves before we can hope to strengthen others, coupled with the feeling of satisfaction that I already comprehended the importance of service, I quickly turned to challenge 11. What would it be about?

As I analyzed what my individual needs were, I yearned to deeply understand the decision-making process and some of the how to's and why for's that would allow me to make my extra effort to become successful.

As I read, I was pleasantly surprised when I discovered Grandfather's insight into the power of positive thinking as it relates to our health and well-being and his insights into necessary changes in our educational system. He gave information not only on how to make proper decisions so we can accomplish our goals, which allows us to serve others, but I was intrigued by Grandfather's in-depth report of statistical data on the problems and challenges facing America's youth. I proudly present Grandfather's challenge 11.

CHALLENGE 11

Decisionmaking Makes It

Dr. Norman Vincent Peale said, "You only lose energy when life becomes dull in your mind. You don't have to be tired and bored. Get interested in something. Get absolutely enthralled in something. Throw yourself into it with abandon. As you do, making up your mind to succeed and calculating the rewards is a natural consequence."

There is nothing more basic to success than learning to make proper decisions. According to Dr. Stephen E. Cosgrove, our life is made up entirely of decisions. In fact, the definition of worry is *not making a decision*. We constantly need to decide yes or no, right or left, now or later and must make our decisions based on knowledge and information. If we make a bad decision it's because either we lack knowledge or we have incorrect information. Remember, everyone is entitled to his or her own opinion, but no one is entitled to the wrong facts!

Get Your Facts Straight!

The other day I was getting my hair cut when the hair stylist said, "Did you know that the Arabs are buying up all the gold?"

I answered, "No, where did you get that information?"

She answered, "From a man who was in here this morning."

I responded, "What qualified him to have that kind of information? What are his credentials?"

She answered, "I don't know."

"And you believed him?" I inquired.

She said, "Sure!"

I quizzed her further. "Do you read the *Wall Street Journal* or other investment periodicals?"

She replied, "No."

"And did you know that the OPEC Arab nations don't seem to believe in investing in gold at all?"

She answered, "No."

I think my point is obvious. We must get our information from reliable sources. It is a proven fact that the man on the street, the woman in the grocery store, and the information in the hair salon are wrong 99 percent of the time.

Time-saving Decisionmaking

Learning to make proper decisions based on correct, reliable, up-to-date information, is critical. Our lives are directly related to decisionmaking, because making a proper decision saves time. If every morning we have to decide whether or not we will take a shower, shave, or brush our hair, we waste valuable minutes. If we take one day and one opportunity to make these decisions, however, then no additional time is ever wasted again. The decision would be made once and for all and wouldn't require a remake each day. Think about how many remake decisions we make day after day about the same things. We perhaps waste one or two hours every day, ten or more each week, five hundred each year, making unnecessary decisions or re-decisions. We'd have a lot more time if we would learn how to gather correct knowledge before the decision and then use it effectively.

Knowledge for correct decisionmaking is gathered from two sources: (1) Personal experience (I must do it or see it done to believe it); and (2) Vicariously (learning from someone else's experiences).

Most of the time we don't have the opportunity to experience something firsthand, but let's not forget that someone else before us has already experienced the same thing. So why do we put so much emphasis on personal experience learning? Of the two decisionmaking sources it seems obvious that vicarious learning (learning from others and then having our own experience) would be the best. Only then can we look back and learn from our past. Let's save time and effort by learning from someone else first. We won't duplicate their mistakes and will be further ahead than if we hadn't listened and learned.

Scouting Reports—For Sports and Everything Else

A perfect example of this comes from the world of sports. How does a football team get ready to play a team they have never played before? They assemble a scouting report. From other games the opposing team has played, they chart the opposing team's tendencies: What do they usually do in this situation or that situation? Do they run or pass more? Who usually carries the ball from the different offensive formations?

An in-depth comprehensive scouting report is very effective and is responsible for most victories. This is nothing more than vicarious learning. Every decision made during the game is made either directly or indirectly because of the report that has uncovered the weaknesses and strengths of the opposing team. We need to also use a scouting report in life—a report from someone who has already played the part of the game that we are now going through. It's a must in developing our skills as effective decision-makers.

If we fail to learn how to gather appropriate information,

we will continue to have to remake decisions. This occurs all the time in business when we hire someone to work for us or when we are thinking about looking for a new job. How many times are we unable to make decisions about employees or a job because we failed to gather all the necessary correct information? Then every day we waste valuable time stewing about the problem: Should he stay; should he go? Should I stay; should I quit? We are miserable until we take time to make a final decision that we should have made in the first place!

Love/Relationships

We can also work through decisions about relationships and marriage with scouting reports. Before we make any commitments, we will save heartache, headache, and part of two individual's lives if we will take time to tabulate facts and figures regarding this important decision. We need to make ourselves aware of all pertinent information. I know this sounds logical, but few follow it. For instance, most Americans are married and seem to like it. But between 1970 and 1980, divorce registered its highest numbers. As we enter a marriage, we should ask ourselves why this is divorce? Only then can we evaluate our prospective partner and see if divorce can be avoided.

Why do people get divorced? National statistics validate: mental cruelty, 40 percent; financial problems, 39 percent; physical abuse, 36 percent; infidelity, 24 percent; drinking/drugs, 27 percent. Divorce is a very miserable and traumatic experience for women more than for men, especially women with children. And the children are usually devastated! Why do we risk marital failure, then, by neglecting to gather information ahead of time to help us make a correct decision?

Have we based our belief and understanding of love on TV romance? Is this TV love portrayed as realistic or fantasy? I believe TV romance distorts the truth about love by teaching us to measure our relate-ability, our sensuality, and our attractiveness by the way we look. It implies to give no thought to commitment. But love is a commitment, not a way of feeling! We need to put and keep the steps of love, therefore, in the proper order. And the proper order is love, marriage, sex. Love and happiness are things you give to, not take from, a relationship. Love grows and comes gradually!

Both partners in a relationship need to decide: Can and will my partner help me become the best that I can be? Can I help my partner become the very best he or she can be? Will we continue to have our individual goals and own lives and individual identities as well as share joint goals and a life of teamwork? There is a big difference between self-fulfillment and selfishness and we must know it and live it! Shall we have children? How many and when? How much money do we need to make? (It doesn't matter how much you make; it matters how much you spend.) Do we agree on a religion or philosophy by which we can raise our children?

As you ponder these questions, realize that in a relationship we spend all of our time and effort trying to sell the product: ourselves. This is especially true before marriage. But for some reason, after we have sold it and finally get married, we stop servicing the product! Let's talk *before* we make the final decision. We don't turn off a marriage like we turn off the lights. Too many of us wait until after we get emotionally involved to ask questions. We marry whom we date seriously, so at some point in the relationship we've got to do some research! When we don't and jump into marriage, most of the time we end up miserable and then just try to ride out our commitment we made when we said I do. Divorce becomes inevitable and we want to "remake" the decision.

Marriage is only one example from life where we need to learn to make correct decisions. And if you're not planning to get married soon, remember that we marry whom we date. Maybe it's time to start examining your friends and relationships for the important ingredients? I belabor the point here to explain something else about decisionmaking.

Emotional Decisions

How often do we blindly jump into something out of sheer energy and emotional stimulation? Decisions should be based on subjective and objective knowledge as well as emotional and factual information, yet about 85 percent of every decision is made based only on emotion. Even when we line up the facts about a person and they don't all properly add up, we still marry him or her because of "good feelings." Is this bad?

Accumulating facts and projecting outcomes based on those facts is extremely important, especially at the beginning of the decisionmaking process, in relationships, in business, in life. This allows our feelings to conceptualize and grow based on nonemotional circumstances. But, after the facts have been gathered, regardless if it's good or bad, we must accept that emotion is nevertheless a major factor in decisionmaking. And because emotion is inevitable, let us look at the good side of it.

Mark McCormack says, "The final decision is more an intuitive process than an analytical one. The danger about relying only on data to make a decision is that we underestimate the importance of intuition—the 'seat of the pants' factor. If you eliminate the need to 'feel' a decision, you won't make very good decisions or you won't make them at all."

One of the most effective ways to develop or rediscover your intuition is to continually ponder: What if? That means instead of taking things as they are, inquire about additional information. Start the question with What if? to stimulate your mind to create new possibilities and alternatives. Don't censor the possibilities, write them down and allow the problem to incubate for a short while. Remember, too much thinking and rethinking of a problem or situation can deter the intuitive process. So, the technique is to place the problem in suspended animation and allow your own instinctual abilities to take over. Then, enjoy the flash of insight. In addition to *What if?* four more words stimulate the intuitive process: *I've seen this before.* If something about a problem or situation reminds you of a previous experience, listen to yourself and trust your judgment. Don't re-invent the wheel. Acquired knowledge and experience equates to wisdom!

Another example of intuition is found in business. A salesperson may present the facts, but the sale isn't made until he or she persuades and emotionalizes the prospective buyer. Each product has its distinctive features, and most of the time we spend our time pointing out the features. But this doesn't sell the product! We need to determine the specific needs of the client and then show how the product meets those needs. For this reason, an understanding of emotional *needs-satisfaction selling* is the key to a successful sales career. Emotion is what makes a person make a final decision, even when facts are present. An executive makes his final decision of whether to hire John or Jim, Jane or Sue, not on the content of their resumes or their high grade-point averages, but on how he *feels* about those candidates. Most Fortune 500 companies hire 85 percent of their new employees on attitude. And how do the hiring executives decide if one applicant has a better attitude than the next? It's an emotional decision founded on the applicant's ability to emotionally sell himself or herself.

Once we get the job, productivity is also a function of good decisionmaking. An increase in personal productivity comes as we eliminate the waste of time and make the proper choice based on prioritization.

The "Cost" of Opportunity Cost

In an economics course we learn about personal productivity as it relates to *opportunity cost,* another ingredient of proper decisionmaking. Here's the best way to explain opportunity cost: There are twenty-four hours in a day. Each of us is exactly equal in this sense. What we do with those twenty-four hours is how we become unequal. We can't do two things at 3:00 p.m., so we have to weigh the pros and cons and make a choice. In this way we are forced to establish priorities before we take action. When we choose one opportunity over another we have to give up one. This is where the cost comes in. As you keep your priorities straight, decisionmaking gets easier as we can literally see the costs and choose the one that positively pays!

I realize some decisions will change as additional information becomes known, and this is acceptable. But many times we are stubborn and feel we can't afford the embarrassment that may come if we change our minds, so we don't change. If this happens, we need to ask ourselves, Do I stay with the decision for the sake of pride, or do I do the right thing and progress ahead?

The answer is simple. Prioritize, weigh the opportunity costs and list the pros and cons of all the variables involved. Then use personal experience and scouting reports to compile the facts. Only now should you make your new decision, and this time it should be more correct. Never be afraid to change your mind if the change is for the best even if you have to endure *sunk costs.* Remember, even in decisionmaking, it's not who's right, but what's right that counts!

Sunk Costs Can Drown You

A western states power and light company had invested 60 million dollars in a new power plant that was presently under construction. But further research showed that the extra electricity the new power plant would provide wouldn't be needed for many, many years, so executives evaluated the situation and halted the project.

It would have been easy for them to say, "We've already put 60 million dollars into it, so we can't stop now." (It was a several-hundred-million-dollar project.) But these sunk costs should not play any part in the new decision. Keep this in mind as we weave our way through everyday life. We can't ever afford to say: In school—"Oh well, I've already blown it and missed class once, so I may as well do it again." In dating—"I've already gone this far, so I may as well go all the way." With drugs and alcohol: "I've already tried this, so I may as well try the rest," or "I may as well finish the bottle before I drive home." Can you see the fallacy in the sunk costs strategy?

To sum up the decisionmaking process, I list the following synopsis techniques:

1. Identify and define the specific problem or decision that you're dealing with.
2. Gather correct information (scouting reports—recall of personal experiences).
3. Brainstorm alternatives with wise people you trust and admire.
4. Predict consequences. (Ask if this, then what?)
5. Check the *forgotten factors* (attitudes, values; feelings, emotions; pressures—peer, advertising, family; risk levels; habits).
6. Choose an alternative plan B (just in case!).
7. Identify an action plan.
8. Act.
9. Evaluate and start over with step 1 if you have to.
10. Persevere until you make the proper decision and solve the problem.

From now on I trust we will put more time and research into our decisionmaking so we will be assured of making the right choices in life. We should always take the pride and the necessary time to get it right the first time! There is no excuse if we don't!

Because the daily choices each of us makes not only affect ourselves but will ultimately affect us all, let us review some of the obstacles our society is now facing to better prepare ourselves to make the best choices possible. To ensure a better tomorrow and a wonderful, productive, educated, drug-free, peaceful world, we need to first identify what is broken. Only then can we decide on the most appropriate solutions. I hate being negative, so let us begin our brief investigation of the problems with a commitment to being positive.

Positive Philosophy Precedes Prosperity

Thoreau wrote, "No one ever rises above that aimed at."

Steve Carlton, Major League pitcher, said, "Man is the only one who puts limitations on himself. There are really no limits. A lot of professional athletes play beneath their ability. They may believe they are giving 100 percent, but they aren't because they are not thinking at their peak. If you so choose, you can create an atmosphere about yourself to become better than your past best performance."

Dan Fouts, NFL Quarterback, explains: "It's hard to separate the mental and the physical. So much of what you do physically happens because you've thought about it and mentally prepared for it."

President Ronald Reagan added to this advice and encouragement when he said, "There is no dream too big for Americans to dream, no goal too optimistic for Americans to pursue. If we roll up our sleeves and get to work, we can turn our problems into opportunities."

It's true. We can turn our lemons into lemonade! No matter how great the obstacle, we can deal with it and overcome it. To win, all we have to do is act as if it were impossible to fail! My dad taught me this: "I can hop over it!"

I grew up on my father's farm. As a twelve-year-old boy I worked hard in the fields, harvesting hay. It was before the invention of the hay baler, so hay was cut by hand and stacked by hand. After the haystacks had dried in the field, my father would drive a wagon through the field accompanied by strong, hard-working men who were hired to walk alongside the wagon. My job was to stomp down the hay in the wagon as it came flying over the edge to make room for more hay. One of the hired hands was a Frenchman with a great sense of humor. He always worked quickly and continuously tried to cover me with hay before I could stomp it. When I was over my head in hay, scrambling desperately to keep up, the Frenchman would laugh and call out, "What did the bullfrog say to the elephant?"

In response, he trained me to answer, "Keep piling it up, big boy, cause I can hop over it!"

It is essential for us to believe in this philosophy of life, especially if we're ever going to be successful. With this positive reinforcement that "what is broken can always be fixed" understanding, let me "pile it up a little." Let's now look at a controversial negative part of the future of America and the World.

The average eighteen-year-old has seen eighteen thousand hours of television. According to the Television Bureau of Advertising, in 1983, households watched an average of seven hours, two minutes of TV a day. Who, then, do eighteen-year-olds and other young people have as role models? How do they perceive the solutions to their problems? How will they get attention? How do they perceive love, sex, family, violence, equality, business and life? Have they been conditioned positively or negatively? How about adults? How have we been programmed? Every seven minutes on network television, alcoholic beverages are being served. Fifteen out of sixteen times it is being accepted—

regardless if it's the good guy or the bad guy. What have we all been conditioned to believe is OK, fun, and necessary in order to deal with problems or celebrate victory? Pretty sick, eh?!

Our society is fast-moving, quick-changing, with millions of people trying to get attention and feel that they belong. This constant desire creates a competitive system wherein sometimes it's difficult to cope. Because we're all different, we try to cope in our own ways. Sometimes it's positive, oftentimes it's negative.

Let's take a look at how the problems with America's youth and schools are changing everybody's world and how these sad statistics relate to challenges that adults have to deal with. As we do, let's recall the conditioning process we've discussed and recommit ourselves to changing negative thinking and actions into positive results. It's a fact that what goes on in our schools always spills out into the community and the work force, and it tarnishes the character of our country. Yes, it does come back around!

We must not isolate ourselves into cliques and groups and say for example: "I'm a senior citizen. I shouldn't have to pay taxes for schools because I don't have children attending them." We need to remember the community togetherness approach and realize that everyone from every age and interest (especially the young people) have an impact on environment and citizenship. It's an ongoing generation-perpetuating-generation circle.

Because this is so important, I now interrupt this challenge to solicit you, the keeper of this sacred writing, to do your own research. I know you will see how times and people are continually changing.

I, Daniel, now interrupt this challenge and add this updated information to this sacred book. In the book *The Battle for the Family,* Tim LaHaye points out a comparison contrast in school environments that points out the drastic changes in our education climate since 1940.

Top Ten School Problems—1940	Top Ten School Problems—1980
1. Truancy	1. Violence
2. Running in the halls	2. Stealing
3. Talking in class	3. Forcible rape
4. Unfinished homework	4. Teacher abuse
5. Loitering	5. Carrying weapons
6. Unreturned books	6. Vandalism
7. Gum in class	7. Substance abuse
8. Talking during study hall	8. Arson
9. Broken windows	9. Rebellion against authority
10. Graffiti	10. Gang warfare

The classroom isn't the only thing affected. The entire school building and all the students are at risk and involved.

In 1984, there were more than 40 million teenagers enrolled in junior high, middle school, and high school.

- 9,000 rapes were committed by those students.
- 12,000 armed robberies were committed by those students.
- 70,000 assaults on teachers were committed by those students.
- 1 million of those students were expelled or suspended from school.
- 600 million dollars were lost to vandalism.
- More than 3,000 prostitutes in Los Angeles, California, were boys and girls under fourteen years of age.

According to the FBI Uniform Crime Reports, in 1984, the following percentages of arrests made nationwide were of people 15 years of age or younger:

- 27 percent of those arrested for murder
- 42 percent of those arrested for rape
- 44 percent of those arrested for robbery
- 44 percent of those arrested for aggravated assault
- 54 percent of those arrested for burglary
- 72 percent of those arrested for arson

Estimated Shifts in the Influences upon Thirteen-to-Nineteen-Year-Olds That Change Their Values and Behavior

1960	1988
1. Mother, father	1. Friends, peers
2. Teachers	2. Mother, father
3. Friends, peers	3. Television, radio, records, cinema
4. Ministers, priests, rabbis	4. Teachers
5. Youth club leaders, counselors, advisors, scoutmasters, coaches, librarians	5. Popular heroes, idols in sports, music
6. Popular heroes, idols in sports, music	6. Ministers, priests, rabbis
7. Grandparents, uncles, aunts	7. Newspapers, magazines
8. Television, records, cinema, radio	8. Advertising
9. Magazines, newspapers	9. Youth club leaders, counselors, advisors, scoutmasters, coaches, librarians
10. Advertising	10. Grandparents, uncles, aunts

According to the National Institute on Drug Abuse, one half of all high-school students have experimented with drugs at least once.

- One third of all high school students are regular users.
- For every teen on drugs, forty more depend on alcohol.

In 1954, the suicide rate of children ten to fourteen years old was 0.3 per 100,000. In 1973, it was 0.7. In those fifteen to nineteen years of age, the rate jumped from 2.4 to 7.0 during the same period. For those in their early twenties it rose from 6.0 to 14.6. In 1988, well over 2.5 million high-school students attempted suicide. Presently,

1 in 10 young people will attempt suicide before they are nineteen years old. Once every ninety minutes an American youth succeeds in taking his or her own life!

What is the bottom line in understanding that comes from these tragic statistics? Now that we know the challenges, we need to start implementing the solutions. We need to be aware of who and what influences our lives. We need to build success into the school curriculum, but we also need to build it into work and play. It's not enough to give someone math homework or a sales job. We also need to teach and show them how to become successful.

Success is defined as getting what we want. For our purposes, let's add to that: *Becoming successful is reliant on our ability to adapt and change to any situation; to be able to graciously win and always learn from our losses; to be able to get up each time we are knocked down; and to be able to dream dreams and use our knowledge and imagination to make our dreams come true.* Most important, success means we have to be given the opportunity to develop our talents and become our best person, not to compete against others, but to discover ourselves and become the best we can be.

Let us now go back into the challenge and garner further wisdom from Grandfather. He expounds on the importance of education reform and seeking to be the best we can be as individuals.

Fable for School People

Once upon a time, the animals decided they must do something heroic to meet the problems of a new world. So they organized a public school.

They adopted an activity curriculum consisting of running, climbing, flying, and swimming. To make it easier to administer the curriculum, all the animals took all the subjects.

The duck was excellent in swimming, in fact, better than his instructor, but he made only passing grades in flying and was very poor in running. Since he was slow in running, he had to stay after school and also drop swimming in order to practice running. This was kept up until his web feet were badly worn and he was only average in swimming. But average was acceptable in school, so nobody worried about that except the duck.

The rabbit started at the top of the class in running, but had a nervous breakdown because of so much makeup work in swimming.

The squirrel was excellent in climbing until he developed frustration in the flying class, where his teacher made him start from the ground up instead of from the treetop down. He also developed a charley horse from overexertion and got a C in climbing and a D in running, which he used to be good at.

The eagle was a problem child and was disciplined severely. In the climbing class he beat all the others to the top of the tree but insisted on using his own way to get there.

At the end of the year, an abnormal eel that could swim exceedingly well and also run, climb, and fly a little had the highest average and was valedictorian.

The prairie dogs stayed out of school and fought the tax levy because the administration would not add digging and burrowing to the curriculum. They apprenticed their child to a badger and later joined the groundhogs and gophers to start a very successful private school.

Since this most edifying little fable was written by G.H. Reavis, the assistant superintendent of public schools of Cincinnati, it causes one to wonder if we're trying to make our kids fit a model arrived at by the educators. I don't wish to be controversial, I only seek to make us think, reevaluate, and strive for "true," realistic, applicable education instead of merely accumulating knowledge.

Let's take the study of algebra for example. I know that many people need a working knowledge of that arcane wizardry; they use it every day in their work. But once we know how to add, subtract, multiply, and divide so that we can handle the business of daily life, do we really need to know algebra if our goal in life is to become, let's say, a writer? Or a champion athlete? Or an attorney or a hotel manager? Maybe now we will realize the importance of vocational organizations and their programs. Not every student needs or even wants to go to college. We need to provide practical education for everyone. College isn't for everyone! Education to provide a good living is what we should be seeking and providing. To return to the fable, must the duck learn to run fast, or the gopher need to fly? I realize human children are not ducks or gophers, but more of them could become eagles if they were permitted to spend more time with their real interests in the area of their major talents. I'm not suggesting anything concrete here, I just want to challenge your belief system! Please let's think about the pertinent issues of real, true, lasting, efficacious education.

Obviously, we have some challenges. But they are not unsolvable. We don't have a curriculum problem in education, business, or anywhere else. We have an attitude problem! And when we can get our attitude problem solved, everything else will fit into place. Remember, when your attitude is right, your abilities will always catch up!

In another book I wrote entitled *Getting High—How to Really Do It,* I made the statement, "We don't learn to know—we learn to do. All the knowledge and information in the world will do us no good unless we can figure out how to use it." It's like the gentleman with three Ph.D.s, one in psychology, one in philosophy, one in sociology. He doesn't have a job, but at least he can explain why!

Positive Thinking: Key to Quality Education

We must build success into the daily curriculum! It doesn't do us any good to know how to read a book if we are not motivated to pick one up and read it. Holistic education and living—combining knowledge with positive-thinking motivation—is the key. It's obvious in business, sales, and education that we can no longer just use current curriculum and training materials because they're not effective by themselves. They never were and never will be! They leave us in the planning/talking/learning stage and never in the action/go/productivity stage. We need motivation—positive input, highly emotional, psyche-up, pump-up, you-can-do-it motivation. Only when we understand this and put it side-by-side with classroom, informational curriculum will we achieve excellence in education, excellence in the family, excellence in business, and excellence in life!

Much has been written about the importance of maintaining a positive mental attitude and how it helps us become successful. I would like to shed some light on this subject from a different angle, in a physiological and medical way.

Emotions Affect Health

Authors throughout the ages have suggested that life is borne more easily with a smile. Plahotep wrote, "Be cheerful and you are alive." This philosophy has survived to the twentieth century and presently covers the spectrum from psychosomatic medicine to biofeedback, explaining the relationship between emotions and physical well-being. This ancient philosophy advocates the power of the mind in fighting off disease. Even though these concepts have been around for centuries, it has been only in the last few years that researchers have confirmed experimentally that the psyche can actually affect the body.

Solid medical evidence reveals a connection between such negative psychological states as depression, stress, pessimism, loneliness, and anxiety to the afflictions of cancer, high blood pressure, heart disease, and other potentially fatal ailments. Stress and negative emotions do not actually cause disease, but they do promote latent disease. The National Academy of Sciences released evidence that grief over the death of a loved one may substantially raise the risk of contracting an infectious disease or of dying of a heart attack or stroke.

The functions of the brain influence the physical state.

How a person feels and how a person sees himself or herself fitting into the world are all critical to physical well-being.

John Liefeskind, a UCLA psychologist states, "I'm fascinated by the possibility that the brain can exert control over the immune system, that our physical welfare might be determined by our mental programming and training." Paul Ekman, psychologist at the University of California at San Francisco, says, "We now know the role that the universal emotions—anger, disgust, happiness and fear—play in health." He concluded that simply moving the facial masks of anger and fear or recreating the mental feeling of these and other emotions can have profound physiological effects: increasing the heartbeat, raising body temperature, and producing other distinctive shifts in the nervous system.

Walter Cannon, in a series of experiments, discovered that several organs and glands—the hypothalamus in the brain, the pituitary gland directly beneath the brain, and the adrenal glands above the kidneys—are all interconnected in a sympathetic nervous system. He explained that when we experience stress, fear, or other negative emotions, these glands prime the heart and muscles for action. We instantly become ready to fight or flee. Eventually this constant gland action breaks us down. I'm not implying that every time we feel stress our immune system weakens and fails. Scientists think that small periodic doses of stress may actually have some benefit. It helps us learn how to deal with our environment more rapidly than we otherwise would.

What I'm saying is that excessive exposure to negative emotion is harmful. It causes a chemical reaction in our bodies that we must fortify ourselves against in our minds. Eisdorfer says, "If we create a way of dealing with the negative event through a positive mental attitude, it decreases our chances of being adversely affected." Continual mental agony causes depressed activity of the immune system's lymphocytes and other white blood cells. This cripples the body's defenses and opens us up to contracting a mental or physical illness.

The body responds in a like manner to positive emotions. They also cause a chemical reaction within us with specific results. As we become positive in our thinking—not occasionally but continually, regardless of the situation—we strengthen our defenses against sickness and disease and cause our organs and glands to manufacture and secrete substances such as endorphin, which stimulate us to overcome obstacles, endure pain, and become our very best.

Positive emotions give us the winner's edge. Positive emotions help us succeed. Positive emotions help us deal with fear, the most common of all negative emotions. Being positive helps us understand that it's not whether you are frightened or not, but whether you or the fear is in control. It's okay to fear; we just need to be able to handle it. Positive thinking helps us manage our negative emotions.

What is the bottom line? If you conquer your mind and conclude to be positive, you'll squash your queasiness.

I, Grandfather, challenge you to accept this philosophy and live by it. May the "force" be with you always as you weather the storm, and may you stay forever young! End of challenge 11.

As a proud, professional teacher, obviously Grandfather needed to expound on decisionmaking as he did in challenge 11. As I re-read it and moved along, I noticed there was only one challenge left. I wondered out of all the things Grandfather could talk about, what would it be? I remember Grandfather always talked about his undying belief in America and our free-enterprise economic system, and, sure enough, this last challenge covered it. He always said capitalism was and will always be the best and most productive system in the world.

Challenge 12 is not wordy but simply an opportunity to unveil his philosophy and the root cause of his loyalties to the USA and its system of success. This challenge, however, was another one of the "You do it, Dan" challenges. Grandfather simply challenged, "Research—Study—Learn—Do and make the capitalistic free-enterprise, incentive-motivation system work for you in your own life. Then record it here in the sacred book for future generations to study and read about!"

Challenge 12 is, therefore, a documentary of my findings and the personal first-hand experiences I have had as a result of taking the time to understand our country, government, and free-market capitalistic system. As you shall see, I, too, conclude and believe that America and its economic system are the best in the world! Until I lived by its principles and tested its teachings, I never realized how fun and exciting the free-enterprise system really is. Enjoy this explanation from my own experience and remember that you too can and should reap benefit from it!

CHALLENGE 12

Free Enterprise—An Age-Old Winner

Jack Lambert, NFL linebacker, said, "The cold wind will be blowing off the lake. It'll be nasty, intense . . . and I'll love it!"

How many times do we hear our employers, parents, or teachers say, "OK, enough fun, let's get back to work." Why do they say this? We need to challenge their statement because work and fun are not mutually exclusive. Ostensibly they could be, but they don't have to be.

Whistle While We Work

Who said work can't be fun?! It's totally up to the individual. For this reason, the free-enterprise system is the greatest economic system in the world. Willie Stargell, major leaguer, said, "Whenever people talk about baseball, they don't say, 'work ball,' they say, 'play ball!' It should be fun."

We all have a choice in what we want to do for a living. Therefore, why not choose something we enjoy doing and "whistle while we work." Why not find a system that allows us to have fun—that creates excitement and fulfillment?

The free-enterprise system, which is a synonym for incentive capitalism, is this kind of system.

It's best because it's the only system that allows us to be free and that forces us to take responsibility for our own actions. It's the best system because it's the only system that requires maturity from its populace to understand that it's not a no-obstacle, no-growth security we want, but rather a high-risk chance-to-get-ahead and become-the-most-productive-we-can-be opportunity for all.

In 1930, Babe Ruth was asked how he felt about President Hoover making less than the $80,000 he was demanding. Ruth's free-enterprise reply was, "I had a better year then he did." Isn't this what we want? Isn't this how it should be?

And in this process of looking for "just" compensations and opportunities, we must decide what we want out of life. For if you think about it, everybody gets what he or she wants. I didn't say each of us has exactly what we need or wish for, but each of us has exactly what we want. Even a wino is successful; he wants more liquor and he always finds a way to get it. Therefore, if you don't like what you're getting, simply change what you want and look at why you want it. The following classic story exemplifies this important principle of free enterprise.

Work for the Money or the Company?

Several years ago, on a hot, balmy day, a crew of men were laying new ties and repairing a stretch of railroad track. It was hard, back-breaking labor. Suddenly a two-car train, pulled by a beautiful engine, came slowly around the bend and groaned to a stop.

It was the company train, custom-made and elaborately decorated. The men stopped work as the door of the last car slowly opened. Out stepped a man immaculately dressed, and in a booming, friendly voice, the man called out, "Dave, is that you?" Dave Anderson, one of the crew chiefs called back, "Yeah Jim, it's great to see you!" Jim invited him aboard for a visit. An hour later, the two men came out, exchanged pleasantries, shook hands, and the train pulled away.

Dave's crew immediately surrounded him for some answers. One laborer spoke up, "Wasn't that Jim Murphy, president of the railroad? How do you know him?"

Dave explained, "Twenty years ago Jim Murphy and I started to work for the railroad on the same day."

Another crewman half-jokingly inquired, "Then why are you still working in the dirt and blistering sun and Jim is the president?"

Dave wistfully answered, "Twenty years ago I went to work for $1.50 an hour and Jim went to work for the railroad."

No Financial Crisis; Only Idea Crisis

Because every person possesses the ability to get what he or she wants and rise to the level of his or her expectations, we need to become acquainted with another incentive-system principle of success. The free-enterprise system also makes true the observation that there is no such thing as a financial crisis; it's only an idea crisis. Ideas create income. All we have to do is select what we want, find out how much it costs, and put together a step-by-step plan to make the necessary money to get what we want. The possibilities are as limitless as are our imaginations. Believe me, I know! A few years ago I had some dramatic opportunities to put this philosophy to the test. Ideas create income!

Porsches and Peepholes

I had had my eye on a sports car for quite some time, a charcoal grey Porsche 911. Because of the high purchase price, I had to carefully plan out my money so I could buy it on the date that I chose—September 11. I'm very time- and goal-oriented.

So for more than six months I had been putting money aside so I could accomplish my goal. On September 1, ten days before the preset purchase date, I realized I was two thousand dollars short. How could I come up with that much money in a week and a half? Well, well, well. Here was my chance to prove the financial crisis versus idea crisis theory. Supposedly, all I needed was an idea, the right idea, and my financial crisis would be solved.

I went to the local hardware store and told the manager about my idea. He loved it and sold me 325 little specially designed brass tubes packaged at a cost of $2.85 each. I purchased a drill bit that perfectly fit the diameter of the brass tubes, grabbed my electric drill, and headed into a neighborhood to try out my brilliant idea.

I knocked on the first door. It opened and a lady and her husband stood in the doorway. I said, "Ma'am, how do you know I'm not a rapist?" Her husband immediately started to flex his neck and walked toward me with his arms quaking. I continued, "I'm not a rapist, so don't worry, but don't you think it would be a great idea if you could see who was on the other side of your door before you opened it?" The woman and her husband both agreed. I said, "Good, because I'm selling these little peepholes (holding up the brass tube peepholes) and I'd like to put one in your door!"

The man gave his OK and asked, "Could you put one in our back door, too?" On that Thursday, Friday, and Saturday, I installed more than three hundred peepholes, made a little more than $2,100.00, and immediately went down and bought my Porsche. Not bad, eh? The "idea" philosophy works!

Rock-Bottom Project

The next weekend I had to prove to myself that my success hadn't been a fluke. I invested about ten dollars in some stencils, purchased some large cans of spray paint, and went into another neighborhood to test out my next idea. I don't know if your neighborhood has the tradition of painting the house address numbers on the curb in front of your house, but this was my new service for sale. And if someone didn't have a curb, I sold them a big rock and painted the numbers on it! If they didn't want a rock, I painted the numbers on the mailbox! There was always a place to paint numbers; all I had to do was use my imagination. Several people I knew drove past in their cars and saw me sitting in the gutter, painting. I could almost hear their conversations just by looking at their surprised faces. They seemed to be saying, "Oh look, Ethel, Dan Clark is in the gutter. When will he ever get a real job?"

I laughed to myself all the way to the bank. Exactly one week from the day I bought my new car, I was completing a second Thursday, Friday, and Saturday sweep. I earned $1,942 painting numbers on curbs and rocks. Hot dog! The "idea" technique worked again!

It's true! There is no such thing as a financial crisis—only an idea crisis. Ideas do create income! They create jobs and breathe life into new businesses. So, if you feel you have a good idea and are contemplating starting a company, let me share some thoughts. The following fifteen points will be helpful to your success.

To start up and create jobs a business must

1. Get an idea that fills a need
2. Design and engineer a product or service
3. Buy materials and facilities to produce it
4. Sell it
5. Deliver it
6. Collect the sales price
7. Pay for the materials and facilities
8. Pay the people who did the work
9. Pay the people who put up the money to start
10. Pay taxes

11. Put enough money aside to do it again
12. Put money away for a rainy day
13. Then start all over again!

And remember that

14. Government regulation and red tape add to the cost of every step except the first and last steps.
15. Ultimately, all costs are passed on to the consuming public.
16. And . . . . if you know something about the business you are going into, and you are willing to invest some of your own time and money into its operation, your chances for success are wonderfully high!

As you try this free-enterprise principle out for yourself, I'm sure you'll also become a believer in *entrepreneurship*.

A major part of entrepreneurship, (an *entrepreneur* is defined as one who organizes or manages and assumes the risks of the business) that must go hand in hand with the good idea is *marketing* (defined as the act or process of selling). Creative marketing can take a seemingly dumb idea and turn it into a gimmick that will sell well.

The hula hoop and pet rock are classic examples. Here is another example: I bought a "Texas cigar" in Houston; it's two feet long. Obviously I'll never smoke it; I'd have to hold it with both hands and feet! I bought it solely as a gimmick to show my friends what I purchased in big Texas.

This theory is proven true time and time again in the entrepreneurial world of the fad makers. A fad or gimmick product is nothing more than an idea—usually a somewhat silly one—that all of us scratch our heads at and ask, why didn't I think of that? Some simple ideas that have created income include the frisbee ($300 million), the hula hoop ($200 million), Cabbage Patch Kid ($250,000 per week and still going strong), the miniskirt ($5.4 million), the smile buttons ($1 million), the pet rock ($5.2 million), the super ball (millions), the ant farm (millions), the Slinky (millions), Silly Putty (millions), Rubik's cube (millions), Trivial Pursuit (over $750 million just in 1986), and the skateboard ($812.5 million).

These dollar figures represent conservative estimates of the product retail sales for the company that first introduced the idea to the public. It's true: ideas create income! So I decided to try out this gimmick idea myself!

A few months after my curb-painting project, I once again started thinking about marketing and entrepreneurship, and now gimmicks. The timing was perfect as I found myself one weekend in Oklahoma. I called one of my crazy friends and he and his wife took me to an arts and crafts fair. His wife was attending some classes and my friend and I got bored just walking around. So we decided to pay the twenty-five-dollar last-day fee and set up shop in an empty exhibition booth. We made a big bright colored sign and hung it up: "Famous Autographs For Sale—$2.00." Almost immediately a long line formed. The girl at the head of the line inquired, "Whose autographs do you have?" I laughed and asked, "Whose do you want?" She replied, "Michael Jackson." I said, "No problem," and took out a beautiful piece of white paper, and signed Michael Jackson. She laughed and paid me the $2.00.

The next person in line said, "I would like Bruce Springstein's autograph." I said, "No problem," and signed an amazing work of art—Bruce Springstein. The next person wanted Boy George. I said to my buddy, "You better sign this one, ha!" That afternoon we not only entertained people and had a few laughs ourselves over a simple gimmick, but together we sold 122 autographs and split our take of $284.

Entrepreneurship Ecstasy

Two weekends later I was in San Antonio, Texas. Again I called one of my fun-loving friends to see how he was doing. Ironically, he and his wife were planning to go to their local fair, so I tagged along for the company. Ted's wife also attended some demonstration classes, so we decided we were going to do something to pass the time. I told Ted about my experience in Oklahoma and he thought it was amusing. We started to brainstorm and got laughing so hard we decided to go and pay the required money to open up a last-day booth at this fair. We found some supplies, made a sign, stapled it across the top of the booth, and started to package our product. I filled the small plastic baggies and Ted drew the labels. We sealed the bags by folding the cardboard labels over the opening of the bag and stapling the sides together. What a professional job— they looked almost store bought! And I'm sure our satisfied customers appreciated our first-class touch.

What did we successfully market? What was the gimmick that made people giggle. What did they buy from us to show what they got in Texas? We took Cheerios, put a few in a baggie, and cleverly sold them for $1.50 as "Doughnut Seeds!" By the end of the day we had developed such a large clientele that we were forced to develop other product lines to accommodate our East Coast and western clients. The same Cheerios magically sold under a new name: "Bagel Seeds." We sold as many of those bags in the first hour as the original product had sold all day. Then we introduced bags of thistle burrs (the little parts of weeds that stick in our socks when we walk through a field). We sold them as "Porcupine Eggs!" That day Ted and I sold 457 bags and split the gross income of $685.50. After expenses, we each cleared $300.00.

Yes, the free-enterprise system works! It's actually fun and exciting! Entrepreneurship works! And my theory on financial crisis versus idea crisis works! The "Doughnut Seed" episode took place in 1984, and I understand that now someone has taken this idea and turned it into a big nationwide money maker! Ideas do create income! And as long as our goals and desires are good, clean, pure, powerful, and positive, we can get anything in life that we want, if we just take the time to understand the principles of the free-enterprise system. Only when we understand it, can we use it to better our lifestyle, buy the things we want and need, make enough extra to feed and clothe the hungry, relieve our government from the financial bondage of welfare, increase our technological advances through competitive inventions, and make the whole world a better place to live.

Boyd and Felice Willat Made a Fortune

In 1980, Felice Willat, on hiatus from her job as a TV production coordinator, took $12,000 of her family's savings to begin a business in the garage. If the location was hackneyed, the idea certainly wasn't. She would eventually produce a glorified date book called "Day Runner" for people as busy as she was.

The Day Runner concept ("it runs your day, it jogs your memory") evolved from Felice's desire to have a journal that kept track of the diverse segments of her life from her job to her personal affairs (from redecorating her home to effectively parenting her three children). Felice's husband, Boyd, a former art director and movie set designer *(Ordinary People, Raise the Titanic),* helped style the book and worked out the technical problems of production. In 1982, he left films to work full-time on the Day Runner.

The Willats christened their business Harper House, after the house on Harper Avenue in West Hollywood where they live and where he had grown up. That first year business was hardly booming, but Felice and Boyd managed to break even on sales of $80,000. Says Felice: "In the beginning, the employees took care of the baby, the dogs, and the garden." The couple themselves put in twelve- to fourteen-hour days; she handled the paperwork and administration while he oversaw production and distribution.

During the next four years, Harper House's sales multiplied spectacularly as Day Runner, which started out with a California following, began to catch on nationally. During the past fiscal year, revenues hit over $15 million with $2 million in profits. Where once only family savings and Boyd's salary could fuel the operations, the couple were now borrowing $700,000 to finance expansion. The work force had risen to fifty-five and taken over every unoccupied bit of space. Lucite displays were assembled in the backyard, orders were shipped from the kitchen, and salespeople made calls from the dining room.

Fortunately, Harper House was as unconventional as the events there. The compound, on two-thirds of an acre, consists of a main house, two smaller cottages, a garage, and an outdoor "boardroom." Initially the Willats employed mostly friends and neighbors. John Bishop, a former music industry producer, became chief financial officer. Says Bishop, "I couldn't believe it. I just happened to be living next door to the best opportunity of my life."

In 1985, Harper House grew too big for its dual mission. The business now occupies a 40,000-square-foot facility.

Capitalism Illiterates?

You can see that an understanding of the basics makes free enterprise rewarding and exciting. But according to surveys conducted by the Princeton Research Institute and the U.S. Chamber of Commerce, many Americans don't understand the barest essentials of our economic system. Fifty percent of America's high-school students can't give even one advantage capitalism has over communism, 67 percent don't believe a business needs to make a profit, and 63 percent think the federal government should own the banks, railroads, and steel companies!

It's apparent that some of these young adults who don't realize the benefits of capitalism will end up living off the welfare system, expecting a handout security blanket from those of us who work. But, as I have observed little kids,

I get excited about the future! All is not lost! I think most of the up-and-coming generation inherently understands basic free enterprise. And it's this generation—our generation—who is going to turn our world around!

Kids Everywhere Are Enterprising

I was in Ireland and attended a meeting with some Jewish associates. One of their young sons (six years old) came up to me after the meeting and we started to talk. He smiled and I noticed he had a couple of teeth missing. I asked, "Did the tooth fairy come?"

He said, "Yeah, and he left me ten pence (about twenty cents) for each tooth!"

I said, "Twenty pence for two teeth—not bad, not bad at all."

A few days later I ran into these same friends. They had all their children with them and this time I started talking with their five-year-old son. I said, "Hey, a few days ago you had a full set of teeth. Now one of them is missing. What happened?"

Without blinking an eye he proudly replied, "I needed the money. I pulled it out myself." Talk about enterprising!

Rebecca's Letter to God

I know of another story where a child taught us a great deal about free enterprise in a democratic setting—specifically the reality of overtaxation and too much government.

This little girl sat down and wrote God a personal letter. It read, "Dear God, I've been a good girl, so please send me a hundred dollars so I can buy me a bicycle. Love, Rebecca."

When the postman saw the letter addressed to God, he didn't know what to do. So he added an address and sent it on to Washington, D.C. When one of the secretaries at a government agency opened the letter, she was touched by the little girl's request. In response, she immediately put a ten-dollar bill in an envelope, addressed it, and mailed it to Rebecca. Rebecca was excited when she received the letter, but was puzzled why it said "Washington, D.C.—Confidential." She quickly opened the envelope and found the ten-dollar bill in it.

In response, she sat down and wrote a thank-you letter. "Dear God, You are wonderful! Thank you for the money. But next time, don't send it through Washington, D.C. They kept ninety dollars of it!" (The United States started a revolutionary war because of high taxes. It's funny I suppose when we stop to ask ourselves, How are we now enjoying our own small taxation?)

Because the more we know the more we can do, let's briefly discuss some other basic free-enterprise principles and practices. Things they possibly forgot to teach us.

Scarcity

In any economics course, *scarcity* is defined as *our wants always exceed our resources.* In other words, what we have never satisfies us; we always want something more.

A Bovine Illustration

A close friend of mine, Charlie Reid, and I were driving in my car in southern Nevada. As we came around a bend in a country road, there, standing by the side of the highway, was a big milk cow. Now, I didn't want to hit the cow, so I slowed down as we passed by. But the cow jumped, so I stopped. As the cow looked in on us, Charlie did something that all of us have done at least once in our lives. He rolled down the window of the car, looked straight into the cow's eyes and bellowed "Moooo!" Now why do we do that? Do we think the cow understands what we are saying or something? But do you know what really cracked me up? The cow looked back into Charlie's eyes, smacked her lips, and said "Moooo" right back. I said to Charlie, "Hey man, do you want me to drop you off or something?"

We pulled the car to the side of the road and watched the cow for a few minutes. As time passed, I began to realize that the cow understood the principle of scarcity. You could see it in her eyes—she wasn't satisfied. She was eating the grass on one side of the fence, staring at the other side and thinking to herself, "The grass sure looks greener on the other side of the fence."

We drove down the road, took care of our business, and came back about two hours later. Sure enough, there was the cow, now on the other side of the fence, eating the grass but apparently still not satisfied. She was staring at where she had been grazing before seemingly mumbling to herself, "No, I made a mistake. The grass is greener where I used to be."

Humans are exactly the same way. We are never satisfied. Poor people want to be rich, rich people want to be famous, famous people want to be powerful, powerful people want privacy. No one is ever satisfied, but that's good! We should like ourselves and the things we are currently doing, but we should always remember we can get better! Scarcity is an important principle to understand.

Other basic prescriptions for success in our free-enterprise society include the understanding of government regulation.

Government Regulation

Government plays an essential and vital role in our free-enterprise system. But in order for capitalism to work, government must never overstep its bounds and interfere where it shouldn't. We need to get and keep most of government out of business! Sure, government definitely plays important roles in food and drug administration, in environmental issues, and in some other appropriate agencies. But, the following role-play illustrates that government regulation should not be found in price controls.

Four students were each given one ballpoint pen, three pencils, and ten pennies. They were allowed to trade and barter for four minutes to see what they could acquire. A lot of excitement was generated as they made deals, bargains, and exchanges according to how much they were willing to pay.

At the end of the four minutes, one student had all four ballpoint pens. She felt they were worth the most at twenty-nine cents each and worked to acquire all four. Another had acquired all the pencils.

Now the rules were changed and the second part of the role-play began. The goods were redistributed with each person again getting an equal amount of each item. But now the "government" stepped in and limited the trading to these circumstances: one pen was worth three pencils, one pencil was worth two cents, etc.

In other words, artificial prices were dictated by the "government." When these price controls were initiated, the excitement of trading decreased until very little trading was going on at all. Instead of making deals and paying the price they wanted, the student had to abide by government rules that fouled up not only supply and demand, but also personal incentive.

When government gets too involved, things get too complicated. For when government makes a decision to assist one group, other groups are usually adversely affected.

Supply and Demand

Another basic principle that most of us already understand is supply and demand. But permit me to review some of the perils of knocking it out of whack. When the demand for a product is high and the supply or production of it is low, the price is relatively high. When the supply is high and the demand is low, the price usually comes down in order to sell the surplus. This is the bottom line of economics. On a graph, where supply and demand meet is where the price is determined. With commodity prices as well as wages!

No matter what the economic system—socialism or capitalism—supply and demand is in effect. Even under communism, where the political system may not let the economy work the way it really should, the principle remains the same. But sometimes the government really messes it up! Instead of letting supply and demand regulate the price for products and wages, the government steps in and dictates a price and a minimum wage. This has happened here in America with the minimum wage laws. Sure, it protects the worker in one respect, but in another respect it causes unemployment. For example, if a company is only producing X amount because the demand is low and finances dictate that it can afford to pay only $3 an hour, how can it be expected to pay close to $5 an hour? How about an unreasonable union demand of $12 or $15 an hour? Wouldn't it be better for the company to negotiate with a worker, decide together on a fair wage, and hire that worker for that wage? The way it is now, the worker is willing to work, but because of government wage laws, the company can't afford to hire him, so he's unemployed.

Supply and demand must be allowed to operate freely in an incentive-based free-enterprise system.

Inflation

A role-play similar to the government-regulation experiment was given to the same group of students so they could see the cause of inflation.

The teacher had three candy bars to auction off to the class. The first bar was auctioned off for real money and went for forty cents to the highest bidder.

Then the teacher passed out some play money and proceeded to auction off the second candy bar. This time, as you can imagine, the candy bar sold for fifty times the original amount.

Notice what happened here. The product didn't change, but when more money was put into circulation, the cost of the bar increased. This happens in real life when the government has a deficit to cover. What do they do to solve their money matters? They print more money to solve the temporary shortage problem, which creates the lasting problem. The government prints more money for circulation, which makes prices go up and the value of money go down. This is essentially what causes inflation! The only way to combat this bad practice of poor money management is to vote for quality politicians who understand this simple point and who will do what's right—not for now but for the long run.

Five Characteristics

With this understanding of several free-enterprise principles now under our belt, let me briefly remind us of the five most basic characteristics of our great capitalistic system. These five characteristics are what make the system work.

1. *Private Ownership of Resources.* An unlimited opportunity for unlimited success, the chance to fail or succeed. Unlike communism or socialism, where resources are government-owned, capitalism allows the individual to own, pay for, and operate his land, tools, and labor. Socialism and capitalism provide security: a roof over your head, food, clothing, and nothing to worry about except work. All you do is show up for work and you're secure.

Capitalistic free enterprise, however, doesn't guarantee this security. Rather, it creates "opportunity" to do what we want, how we want, whenever we want, and to make as much money as we want. Private ownership of resources allows us to set goals and exceed them, to earn an honest day's pay for an honest day's work, and to discover our potential in life and succeed in fulfilling it. Private ownership of resources is best explained with the example of young teenagers owning their own cars. When teens own their own cars themselves, they don't squeal the tires, screech the brakes, or abuse them. Economically speaking, private ownership creates an incentive motive to not only take better care of the resources, but to take more pride in the quality of production and more personal interest in proper beneficial decisions that affect the resource.

2. *Self-Interest Motives.* An individual should be motivated to do things for himself, and as he or she does so, all will benefit. Someone hated food stuck in his teeth, so because of self-interest, he invented the toothbrush, and everyone benefited. Someone else spotted a need in grass yards everywhere and invented the lawn mower to satisfy that cutting need. Profit is basically goal-generated by self-interest motives. Profits represent to the system what satisfaction of biological needs represent to the human being. Without food or water (self-interest) the individual dies. Without profits (self-interest) the business cannot survive.

A person motivated to make more money is also motivated to make a better product to increase his sales volume. He is motivated to increase production, which increases the number of jobs available, which makes him more profit. This allows him to produce more tax dollars which builds more schools and pays teachers to educate more students so they can make profits and start the self-interest motive cycle over again.

3. *Consumer Sovereignty.* You've got to produce a product or provide a service to fill a specific need. You've got to effectively supply the demand, know what consumers want and need, and gear your thinking and actions accordingly. Remember, the consumer is King!

4. *Markets.* The market is the place where we trade, buy, or sell our goods and services. And if there is no particular present market for our goals and success, we can create one! The free-enterprise system is an incentive market system curtailed only by our supply-and-demand imagination to satisfy a need. A free-market system allows us to honestly wheel and deal where and when we want and

rise to the level of financial success that our education and working skills will allow.

5. *Competition.* Fair and open competition is the primary regulator of the market. Not a dog-eat-dog competition for survival but a healthy competition that regulates itself. The consumer shops for the best quality at the best price. This creates competition among businesses to meet the public demand and develop a worthwhile product at a lower cost, benefiting all and in fact regulating itself. The producers can sell a product only for what the consumer is willing to pay. Competition benefits the company because new technology, better production methods, and improved product quality result. The consumer benefits in both product quality and lower price paid.

Competition is best explained in a sports setting. You'll notice that the basketball team that wins the world championship is the one with the best bench—the best second-string players. On any other squad, these players would be starters. But on the championship team, they are the competition that inspires and forces their first-string teammates to work harder and be the best they can be.

What do the former explanations of scarcity, government regulation, supply and demand, and inflation boil down to? And what do these five characteristics of free enterprise help us understand?

Free Enterprise

Anthony Harrigan explains,

> In a free enterprise system, an individual has the right to sell or exchange his property and/or labor for the best bargain he can make. Under free enterprise, private property means that everyone is free to retain the fruits of his labor and put them to any lawful use he sees fit.
>
> Free enterprise also is based on the principle that only a working society can survive. People must help support their community and nation. They can't lead a welfare existence, dependent on the work and savings of others. Yet many liberal

politicians ignore the rights and needs of productive working people and lavish benefits on the lazy and those who don't know the meaning of thrift. The free-enterprise system, in order to work, must be free of both government coercion and economic restrictions.

Free enterprise means just that—free to enterprise—free to negotiate on our own behalf if we so desire, free to work for a reasonable wage, and free to keep our profits, which motivates us to be financially successful day after day, year after year.

The Real Cause of America's Economic Crisis

According to the *Book of Lists,* "Tight money, federal budget deficits, foreign imports, and decreased productivity have been blamed for the current economic problems being faced by the U.S. However, the real cause of the deterioration of our economy is the disappearance of truly competitive economy. Monopoly, militarism, multinationalization, and unreasonable unions have destroyed the free-enterprise system and created inflation, stagnation, and unemployment."

We have established that the American capitalistic system is simple to understand, interesting to learn about, and rewarding to work with. It's also fun to live in! Compared to other systems, it is the most positive and productive, exciting economic system in the world.

For these reasons, let us now shift gears into political and idealogical differences and commit to do some in-depth additional research on your own. Take time to discover for yourself that I am not an alarmist but only reporting the facts. Take time to educate yourself and form your own opinion about the following true, non-biased facts.

Fascism, Communism, Capitalism: You Decide Which Is Best

If a person has a cow, the fascist takes the cow and kills the person. The communist takes the cow and sells you the milk. The capitalist saves some money from selling the milk, buys a bull, and has more cows. This is a clever way of explaining the philosophical discrepancies of three different governments. But let us put these principles into real-life practice. How do the communist officials think and perform?

We don't ever want to live under fascism or communism! History proves that under communism, human life means nothing. Lenin said, "What is it to kill nine-tenths of a population to purify the one-tenth." Khrushchev yelled at America, "We will bury you." Karl Marx said, "The end justifies the means." In other words, communists believe that whatever they have to do to reach world domination is acceptable. When Stalin came to power in the Soviet Union, he threw thousands of people in prison just because they had relatives abroad. Between 1917 and 1950, Stalin and Lenin slaughtered over fifty million Russian citizens because of their political or personal beliefs.

Recently, a friend of mine finally got out of Russia and explained a few confidential things to me. He was forced to wait six years from the time he applied until the time he was finally permitted to leave. All the communist newspapers print exactly the same government-regulated propaganda. Every person is required to get a photograph identification-card passport when he or she turns sixteen years old. Everyone must report each move to the police before doing it—a family picnic and a visit to relatives are no exception! And if you move from one place to another, you have only three days to report this to the authorities or you are thrown in jail for one year. When you get a job—the one the government selects for you—officials record it in a master book and continually chart your progress. If you do something wrong, it's recorded and you are always on file as a troublemaker. Farmers don't get paid until the end of the year. Then the government decides how much to pay them.

Alexander Solzhenitsyn estimates that 66 million dissidents have been imprisoned in forced-labor camps, and that the U.S.S.R. leads all nations in the world in crimes against human rights. Some defenders of communism agree there were crimes committed years ago, but they say it doesn't happen today. You tell me! In 1969, the communists took over Cambodia. At that time the population of Cambodia was about 8 million. *Time* magazine recently reported that today the population is 4 million. They discovered that over half the population was killed. The new communist government killed the educated, which allowed them to reeducate the masses with communist propaganda. Am I overdoing it a little? No! We Americans have been lulled to sleep about the crimes of aggression committed by Soviet leaders and their ultimate world-control intentions. We think they surely must be exactly like we are. To the contrary! The Soviet citizens are literally brainwashed to think just like their leaders.

Communism Cowardice

Sure, only 5 percent of the Soviet population are members of the Communist Party, but the rest are wary and afraid to rise up against it. They know it's a stone wall! This is why we should all be concerned about communism as it relates to our foreign policy. Especially concerned when all we see at home are "peace marches." It's true and important—we all want peace. But we should want freedom more! Inmates in prison have peace but no freedom! A woman tied up in chains has peace but not freedom! A person in a communist country has peace but is not free to choose, to go to work, to play. Yes, we want peace, but we will never enjoy peace without our freedoms!! And when someone or some government wants to take freedom away, yes, we should fight to keep it!

Sure, we don't want war but that doesn't mean we should be afraid when dealing with the Soviet Communists. In a study of more than one thousand treaties, researchers discovered that the Soviets are the champion treaty breakers of all time. Most countries felt secure at one time—until the Russians decided to make their world domination plans come true and either break a treaty or implement a communist takeover. Ask the Poles (1939), Estonians (1940), Lithuanians (1940), Latvians (1940), Germans (1945), Yugoslavs (1946), Czechs (1948), Bulgarians (1948), Hungarians (1949), Tibetans (1951), North Koreans (1953), Vietnamese (1954), Cubans (1959), Cambodians and South Vietnamese (1969), Afganistanis (1980—sure, they have pulled out, but think about the sorrow and devastating harm they left behind!) Now they all are "captive audiences." The Soviets have never—I repeat, never—kept a treaty with the U.S., either. So why do we keep thinking they will change?

When you deal with the Soviets, you are dealing with a leadership that has been mentally conditioned completely differently than free Americans. A Soviet leader does not believe in a supreme being and does not value human life. To him, human beings are just objects with no purpose for living or hope in life after death. Human beings, therefore, have no inherent, inalienable rights. They are, in every sense of the word "used" only as workers, fighters, and pawns simply for the good and common goal of the government. If you won't do as they say, they just get rid of you by killing you or throwing you into prison. Thousands have been slaughtered in Afghanistan, South Vietnam, and in every other country they have invaded. Thousands of Jews and political dissidents are currently being persecuted in Russia and other communist countries.

Communists believe that what is theirs is theirs, but what is yours is always open for negotiation. They look upon a treaty as a simple piece of paper until you break your side of it. Look at Detente and Salt I, and especially Salt II. The only reason the Soviets wanted to "negotiate" in 1985 was because President Reagan had spearheaded a defense buildup over the previous five years and had announced the Star Wars plan. So why do the Soviets suddenly want to talk treaties? All they're doing is trying to buy time so they can steal more technological secrets and catch up with us again!

Some say our defense strategy and strength philosophy is bad. No, it's good—it's working. My insurance salesman's pitch explains why: "It's better to have it and not need it than to need it and not have it." It's much safer and easier to negotiate with the Soviets from a position of strength than from a position of weakness. America's defense needs to be strong! Building more nuclear warheads is ridiculous and spending billions on other weapons seems crazy, but what do we do?

Before we start spouting off with protests about this and that, let us learn the facts. And as we do, I hope and pray along with Sting, who wrote, "I hope the Russians love their children too."

Economics

We have talked politics and military—let's talk economics. The chart on the following page speaks for itself.

Capitalism, Socialism and Communism

Wilson S. Johnson, president of the National Federation of Independent Business, said, "The economic system which serves its people best provides maximum freedom and opportunity, furnishes the greatest amount of goods and services at the most reasonable prices and in terms of money or time worked, it definitely brings the highest quality of life possible to all its people." The following chart will allow you to decide which economic system is best and fits all of the aforementioned criterion.

Comparative Standard of Living

Approximate work time required for an average manufacturing employee to buy selected commodities in retail stores in Washington, D.C., and London, and at state-fixed prices in Moscow during 1976 (compiled by the National Federation of Independent Business).

COMMODITY	WASHINGTON, D.C.	LONDON	MOSCOW
White bread (1 kg.)	21 minutes	10 minutes	20 minutes
Hamburger meat, beef (1 kg.)	34 minutes	76 minutes	3.5 hours
Sausages, pork (1 kg.)	71 minutes	60 minutes	2.6 hours
Potatoes (1 kg.)	8 minutes	23 minutes	7 minutes
Apples, eating (1 kg.)	16 minutes	24 minutes	5.4 hours
Sugar (1 kg.)	9 minutes	15 minutes	65 minutes
Milk (1 liter)	7 minutes	11 minutes	21 minutes
Eggs (10)	10 minutes	13 minutes	97 minutes
Vodka (0.7 liters)	67 minutes	3.4 hours	9.8 hours
Cigarettes (20)	10 minutes	27 minutes	23 minutes
Weekly food basket for four people	17.2 hours	28.2 hours	64.6 hours
Soap, toilet (150 gms.)	5 minutes	10 minutes	72 minutes
Lipstick	31 minutes	54 minutes	7.8 hours
Panty hose	18 minutes	15 minutes	9 hours
Men's shoes (black, leather)	6.7 hours	7.7 hours	36 hours
Man's business suit	25 hours	40 hours	106 hours
Refrigerator, small (150 liters)	47 hours	50 hours	168 hours
Color TV set, large (58 cm. screen)	3.9 weeks	5.5 weeks	19.15 weeks
Small Car (Fiat or Zhiguli)	6.9 months	11.1 months	3.1 years

America's "Melting Pot" of People

We should realize that America is the greatest country in the world; others seem to think it is. No one is climbing walls and barbed-wire fences trying to get into Russia, or East Germany, or any other communist country. Instead, people are trying to escape from those countries! Immigration to America has been unbelievable. Between 1890 and 1930 more than 16 million individuals, averaging thirty years old, entered the U.S. through New York City alone! In just the month of December of 1907 more than one million people immigrated to America. That's more than thirty thousand per day. Why? And why does Neil Diamond now sing about "Comin' to America?" Because they're still coming! The Statue of Liberty's message is, "Give me your tired, your poor, your huddled masses yearning to be free."

They come because we have more than 107,000 schools and 700 colleges and universities. They come because in America you can be who you want to be. They come because we believe in capitalism and practice the free-enterprise system where anyone can grow, develop, and get ahead if they work hard. Sure, you may fail—but then, again, you may succeed! The Asian boat people are a classic example of success in America. While most Americans are taking our country and our opportunities for granted, these Asian immigrants are grateful for and humbled by the chance to live in the greatest country on earth. And they don't want to waste any time catching their part of the American dream. Statistics show that within one year after they arrive in the states, just under 100 percent of them are working. More than 75 percent have already started their own businesses, and this is when they barely speak English! Their children are even winning math contests and securing academic scholarships in prestigious schools! Should we get upset at the competition? No! Free and fair competition in the marketplace is one of the principles that makes America the land of the free, the home of the brave—the greatest country in the world. Only in America can economic miracles happen. Only in a capitalistic free-enterprise system can we make our economic and technological dreams come true.

I conclude this challenge with a short address delivered over CBS radio by my uncle, J. Reuben Clark, an outstanding father, world religious leader, rags-to-riches businessman, solicitor general for the United States State Department, and former U.S. ambassador to Mexico. Presented before the United States Senate, it passed by unanimous consent and was printed in the *Congressional Record*. Whether we're rich or poor, minority or majority, male or female, bound or free, Catholic or Protestant, Jew or Gentile, Muslim or Hindu or Buddhist, liberal or conservative, we all have a common denominator: we're Americans. In this cause we are one! In this way, we all have the same last name. We're Americans and I believe my uncle speaks for all of us as he capsulizes what this challenge is all about.

I Am an American

I am an American because I believe in a government with three distinct, separate branches, each mutually independent of the other, with no power of delegation or appropriation of rights or powers by any one to or from any other.

I am an American because I believe that government "must derive its just powers from the consent of the governed" and that branches of government and officers shall have such powers only as shall be given by the people.

I am an American because I believe in the greatest possible measure of self-government and because I believe in a federal system of government which keeps local affairs in the hand of local governments.

I am an American because I believe in a Bill of Rights which places wholly beyond the reach of lawful government certain matters affecting "life, liberty, and the pursuit of happiness," and specifically the right of freedom of conscience and worship, the right of free speech and a free press, the right peaceably to assemble and petition government, and the right to gain and hold property without molestation except by due process of law.

I am an American because under our form of government the people of the United States have made a progress never before made by any other people in the world in an equal time during the whole period of recorded history.

I am an American because standards of life and of living of the entire American people are far beyond those enjoyed by any other people in any other part of the world, either now or at any other time, which is a living testimony and evidence of the kindly beneficence of our free institutions.

I am an American because this nation has no scheme or plan of conquest, because it has a respect for the rights of other peoples and of other nations, because it promotes justice and honor in the relationships of nations, because it loves the ways of peace as against war, as shown by the repeated peaceful adjustment of its own international disputes.

I am an American because my country acknowledges the equality of all races, abolished slavery after it had become deep-rooted so that men and women are still free to work, and because we are secure in the enjoyment of the products of our labors.

I am an American because I firmly and earnestly believe that the Constitution is an inspired document designed by our Maker to set up a government which would make sure and secure the rights set forth in the Bill of Rights, and particularly the right of freedom of conscience and worship.

I am an American because I believe that the destiny of America is to be the abiding place of liberty and free institutions, and that its own practice and enjoyment of these blessings shall be to the world a beacon light which shall radiate its influence by peaceful means to the uttermost parts of the world, to the uplifting of all humanity.

Yes, America with its capitalistic free-enterprise system is the greatest country on earth. Therefore, let us be honest and look inside. If you don't feel as if you're doing your part to support our freedom values; if you're not building our system and keeping America Number One, please recommit and catch the spirit of the United States of America. Sure, we have problems and things that aren't all right. But that's what makes America so great! We are allowed to work hard to change what is not right and fix what is broken! If you complain but refuse to get involved in the changing process, do as the old bumper sticker states, "Love It or Leave It!" I promise you that our system will work for you as you work for it. America needs you! You're one reason America is great. And as you participate more and get more involved, you'll make America better than she's ever been before! As Lee Greenwood sings so well, "I'm proud to be an American . . . I love this land . . . God bless the U.S.A."

I, Daniel, under the direction of Grandfather Clark and by the power of the great Kahuna invested in me, challenge you to accept this philosophy and live by it. May the "force" be with us always as we weather the storm, and may we all stay forever young! End of challenge 12.

EPILOGUE

There you have it. Grandfather's twelve challenges on how to love life, living, and the pursuit of happiness. Twelve philosophies that instruct and remind us of what matters most. Twelve clearly stated explanations on how and why every human being is engineered for accomplishment, endowed with the seeds of greatness, and yet supposed to fail our share of the time. Twelve revelations that teach successful living is an opportunity, not a guarantee; that we should not wait for life to happen to us—we must happen to life; that true happiness and lasting successful satisfaction comes in the journey—not in the destination. Twelve reminders that the difference between good and great is just a little bit of extra effort.

Yes, each and every person truly can and will ultimately overcome every obstacle and endure every tribulation if we will just weather the storm!

And it won't be easy—believe me, I know! I am proud to present the world these twelve challenges because I have been an expert eyewitness to the practical application power found within them. Yes, believing in and following these teachings literally saved my life. I conclude this book with my own personal testimony that "stuff" happens, but you were born to succeed, so weather the storm!

My testimony of weathering the storm is found in an elementary quotation: "You can if you think you can." Herein lies the key! But, you must read it correctly in order to understand it correctly. Proper pronunciation accents: You can only if *YOU* think you can!

Because success and failure always boil down to individual self-belief, self-discipline, self-motivation, self-effectiveness, and personal perseverance, the only difference between success and failure lies in the six inches between our ears!

If you feel you have been failing more than your share of the time, maybe it's simply because you've expected to fail. Remember, when we get hurt, the doctors don't heal anyone. They only give us medication or perform surgery to help us heal ourselves. The power is within! The power to succeed or fail is also found within. Success came from within for me! And yes, it will come for you, too! As the challenges teach us, all we need to succeed has been inside each of us since birth. Each of us is already fully equipped to succeed! All we have to do is open up, dig deep down, and pull out the necessary inner talents and tools that we need to solve our problems and make our dreams come true!

If your personal powers have been lying dormant inside of you, sitting untapped as an undiscovered oil reserve, why not drill a well and let the oil (your ultimate capacity and potential as a human being) out where it can be used as it was meant to be used.

Dan's Own Story

Please forgive the following experiences, if recounting them seems self-serving, but it is the reason why I spend my time writing, singing, and speaking about hope, happiness, and getting high naturally.

Coming out of high school I had the opportunity to play some big-time baseball. But, because of family advice, I decided to pursue a professional football contract and accepted a full athletic scholarship to play baseball and football at the University of Utah. Why Utah? I was one of the many fools who followed my girlfriend to college! The second I signed my letter of intent, binding me to go to the University of Utah, my girlfriend and I broke up and I was stuck there. (This had a lasting effect on my destiny and taught me that I need to take care of the person who is going to be at my funeral for sure, and then pack the mortuary later!)

I hung in there and fell in love with the prestigious university (world famous for its medical school, engineering school, amazing snow and ski resorts, and over 25,000 friendly, first-class students). Time passed and my dream of playing professional football was coming true.

I had been playing football for thirteen years, when one day in practice the dream ended. I was the biggest I had ever been (6'5", 257 lbs.), the strongest I had ever been (bench pressing 400 lbs.), and the fastest I had ever been (4.6 40-yard dash). But, one moment in time stopped the dream and suddenly shoved my life into a depressing downhill slide that would eventually hit rock bottom and lead me to a plot to commit suicide.

The first day of football practice, we, the players, were lined up into two equal lines for a tackling drill. My favorite part of the game was the physical contact, the hitting. (Once in a game where we were losing by twenty points, I called time out with five seconds left on the clock just so I could get one more legal hit on the "jerk" offensive lineman playing across from me!)

This tackling drill was the first competitive exercise of the year and our adrenaline was high. The coach spread the two lines thirty feet apart (a real dumb idea!) and blew his whistle. Two of us ran into each other full speed. The only parts of our bodies that made contact were Lyle's helmet and my right shoulder. We fell to the ground. When Lyle got off of me, I noticed that my right arm was totally numb, I was numb all the way up into my face, my right eye drooped, and I had loss of speech. I couldn't talk anymore. The coach and trainer came running over, "Clark, Clark, are you OK?"

I replied, "Rassa, Baboo, snitchel fart!"

The coach smiled and countered, "You've got serious problems. You better come over here and sit down."

I said, "Roof!"

A doctor who was present on the field came over to examine me. He pulled the coach aside: "Clark has serious nerve damage. In fact, he might even have serious brain damage!"

The coach asked, "How will we ever know?" (Nice guy!!)

I stayed like that for two hours. Finally my eye went back to normal and my speech came back, but my right arm stayed totally numb, dangling helplessly at my side. I talked to it—it wouldn't move! It scared me to death!

I eventually went back to school, but as I walked down the halls my arm just dangled there. I put my hand in my pocket and it still dangled there. I went to another doctor and he put me into an invention called an "airplane splint." It consisted of two big metal braces that wrapped around my chest with a metal bar that propped my right arm up and out my side. Oh perfect! Now I looked like a one-armed motorcycle rider and when I passed by friends in the hall they called out "vrooom, vrooom, vrooooom!" In class, I leaned back in my chair to stretch, my arm in the splint shot up and the teacher said, "Yes, may I help you?" What a drag! I went home and took it off. The splint wasn't working, anyway.

I started getting little electrical impulses in my shoulder that caused my arm to uncontrollably "flip out." I went to a family dinner and as I was sitting at the dinner table, suddenly my arm went "wing!" It shot out and knocked a bowl of mayonnaise off the table about twenty feet. It frightened everyone and at the next meal, my younger brother showed up wearing a helmet and goggles! He bobbed and weaved at the end of the table yelling, "Please pass me the bread!" What a drag!

I remained paralyzed for two years. Sixteen of the best doctors in America all had differing opinions and different concepts of therapy. I did what they said, it didn't work, and they were baffled. None of the physical therapists I religiously went to could help me either! I had severed the auxiliary nerve in my right deltoid, severely strained my brachial plexes and super spinadois and most likely suffered from some shock and possible scar tissue irritation from my broken 7th cervical vertebrae, which I had fractured earlier. The only thing the doctors could agree on is that I only had a 10 percent chance of recovery! Needless to say, my depression slid deeper and deeper. The light at the end of my tunnel was quickly fading and I seriously contemplated suicide.

Sure it was a physical injury, but it effected my entire life. I couldn't write anymore (I was right-handed). I couldn't concentrate on doing my homework anymore; my shoulder hurt too much. Obviously, I couldn't throw a baseball anymore. I continued to play football, however, but the only way I could play was with my right arm strapped to my side. Now, picture yourself as the opposing team's quarterback: McMahon gets the ball, looks up and sees me chasing him down the field with my hand flapping up and down at my side. (It looked very effeminate and scared him to death! Maybe that's why his hair sticks straight up!) I finally hit an all-time low and didn't know what to do. I cried out for help but real help never came. I did, however, learn about friendship.

Ask yourself, What is a real friend? A lot of us think a friend is someone we've known for a long time—a person we do things with. That's not a friend—that's an acquaintance. We all have acquaintances.

A real friend is rare and may come around only once

or twice in a lifetime. A real friend is someone who runs in when everyone else is running out! A real friend is someone we can totally trust; someone who likes us for who we are, not for what we look like; someone who doesn't expect us to change our hairstyles, health habits, clothing, and moral standard just to fit into a certain clique, someone who believes in us when we won't; someone who accepts us but knows we can get bigger, better, faster, stronger, smarter, and therefore, gently invites us to grow! Yes, a real friend always has a positive influence on our lives and conducts himself or herself in a positive way so we always say when we are away from him or her, "I like me best when I'm with you—I want to see you again!"

Do you know any friends like this? Have you ever been this kind of friend? Are you a positive influence on others, or do you gossip and put others down to make yourself feel higher and better about who you are? Are you a big thinker or a pessimistic small thinker who's actions say to peers, "Let's stick together and drag each other down"?

I make an issue out of friendship because when I hit rock bottom and became so depressed that I didn't think I could go on anymore, that's when I discovered who my real friends were!

When I was down, a so-called friend came up to me and said, "Hey, Clark, you're paralyzed, eh? No more Raiders? Let's go get drunk."

Think about this! You're down and somebody wants to keep you down? That's not friendship—that's selfishness! We don't need those kinds of friends! I wouldn't be here today if I had followed this "friend's" advice! Have you ever been this kind of "friend"? Do you know anyone who is? You're desperately hurting, down and out looking for help, and the only suggestion they have is a Band-Aid to anesthetize the pain for a while!

I had another so-called friend come to me and say, "Dan, you're paralyzed, eh? Your life is falling apart, eh?

Let's go get stoned. Let's go have a good laugh—forget about it. Let's get high and do some drugs!"

Think again! You're down and somebody wants to keep you down? That's not friendship—that's selfishness! We don't need those kind of friends! They only want to get us artificially high for a minute, but where will they be when we come down and they go home and we are left alone, lonely, still hurting, and more depressed than we were before?

The basketball coach Bobby Knight of the University of Indiana was talking to the top high-school basketball players in America. While talking about drugs, he told them, "Say no. It's easier to turn no into a yes, than a yes into a no. Why say no?" Bobby Knight continued. "In the last ten years, the two very best men's college basketball players to play the game are Michael Jordan and Lenny Bias. Michael Jordon is a superstar, making $5 million a year playing professional basketball for the Chicago Bulls of the NBA. Lenny Bias is dead! Michael Jordan has been Rookie of the Year, MVP of the league, has won the slam-dunk contest many years in a row, and gets high naturally. Michael Jordan has never ever done drugs. They have never touched his lips! Lenny Bias is dead! Michael Jordan was in control of his destiny and chose to be a superstar. Lenny Bias was in control of his destiny and chose to die! Lenny Bias didn't sprain his ankle or blow out his knee so that he can recover. Lenny Bias is dead and gone— never to play again."

Len Bias, the University of Maryland basketball star and number-one draft choice of the Boston Celtics (an overnight millionaire at the age of 22), died of a cocaine overdose. And the saddest part of this story is, Bias didn't buy the coke himself. He got it from a so-called friend! Where is that friend now? I had a friend drink and drive and kill three of my friends in his car. What kind of a friend was he? What kind of a friend have you been? What kind of a friend are you now and will you be? Are you a positive influence or a negative influence on others? Do your friends really, truly want to be around you and see you again?

Back to my story. I was down and out for over two years. I cried out to my "significant others" and received no positive help. I decided to kill myself. My friends' suggestions only brought me down further. Then I met two real friends. One was a doctor whom I didn't know very well. Yet, he became a "real friend" because he gave me medical hope and support that I could recover from my paralysis. His name was Dr. Brent Pratley—one of the very best orthopedic surgeons in the world. I believed and appreciated his optimism, which allowed me to once again believe in myself.

The second real friend I found was Mr. Norman Gibbons, the dean of students at the University of Utah (notice how many times I have quoted him in this book.) When I was depressed, he simply befriended me and gave me a cassette to listen to. It was a recording of a speech given by a motivational speaker by the name of Zig Ziglar. I had never heard of him before. I intently listened to Zig's message and it literally changed my life. (We have since become good friends. He was my sponsor in the National Speakers Association in 1982 and has called my father several times during his bout with cancer. Zig is my hero!) His positive words of hope and hard work didn't change my paralyzed arm—it still dangled there. But his words did change the way I looked at my injury. As Zig would say, he "gave me a checkup from the neck up to eliminate hardening of the attitudes." He seemed to be speaking directly to me and simply said, "The power to succeed and overcome tremendous obstacles is stuck inside of you. You just need to get it out where you can use it." He encouraged me to stop feeling sorry for myself and take the first step in a positive direction to make myself better today than I was yesterday.

I believed Zig and realized for the first time since my injury that success wasn't moving my arm all the way above my head, but rather moving it an eighth of an inch farther than I had moved it before. And, just maybe, if I could move it an eighth of an inch, I could move it another and another eighth of an inch. Suddenly, this was something I realistically thought I could do!! Zig Ziglar's words empowered me to concentrate more and work harder than I had ever worked before. I locked my door with the commitment and attitude of mind that I wasn't going to come out of my room until I got my hand above my head. I started the struggling process.

I struggled and raised my hand an eighth of an inch. (Amazing how we rise to our expectations and no higher!) I immediately propped my arm up so I wouldn't have to raise it that high again. I rested, regained my energy and strength and again fought, struggled, and sweated to lift my arm up higher. I again propped it up so I wouldn't have to raise it that high again! I rested, regained my energy and strength and again concentrated all of my human capacity to lift my arm higher. Again I propped it up. I had pillows, shoes, books, clocks, you name it, but seven hours later my hand was above my head. I did it!

The next day I followed the same process, an eighth of an inch at a time, and it only took me five hours. I was making progress!! I continued on until I could eventually raise my arm up ten times in a row. Then I went into the weight room where I could take a 5-pound, a 10-pound, and a 25-pound weight and lift it with my extended arm ten times. Over the course of six months I got the complete and total use of my arm back.

It's interesting. All the feeling has come back into my arm, but my shoulder is still totally numb. The nerves never grew back. And you have to have nerves in order to contract and flex the muscles and make them move correctly. Doctors can't really explain how I do it, physical therapists don't even have a clue, but I don't even care! It works!!

Sure, I can't play professional football or baseball, but

I have full range of motion and effectively compete against those whom I play! And it has taught me a great principle of life that we need to remember: "stuff" happens! So what are we going to do about it? I trust we will weather the storm! Each of us is in charge of our own destiny. Therefore, "It's better to shoot for the stars and miss than it is to aim for a pile of manure and hit!" We owe it to ourselves to go for it!

Each of us was definitely born to succeed. The question is, Will we or won't we? Work will win when wishing won't! The only thing we are not in charge of is whether or not we are in charge! No matter what our past has been, we *have* a spotless future! Therefore, go for it! Reach your ultimate capacity and potential as a human being! Strive for perfection and in the process attain excellence! Never say never! Learn to laugh, and don't worry—be happy!

I, Daniel Mark Clark, grandson to Grandfather Samuel Clark, by the power of the boomerang invested in me, challenge you to accept all of the philosophies and challenges I have transcribed from the sacred book. They have been recorded herein, and I challenge you to live by them *now*!!! As you do, I guarantee that you will become everything you were born to be! May the "force" be with you always as you weather the storm, and may you stay forever young!

The end. (Which is the beginning!)